Bill Bernhardt teaches at the City University of New York (CUNY), where he is an Associate Professor of English at the College of Staten Island and the School of Professional Studies. He has also taught at Fisk University and Reed College in the U.S., Keele University in the U.K. and Hebei Teachers University in China. He has conducted seminars in the teaching of writing in many countries throughout the world including Brazil, France, and Vietnam.

Despite many years of formal academic study in the U.S. and U.K., as well as extensive reading in many fields, he feels that his training as a teacher only began in earnest at the age of 34, when he came under the influence of Caleb Gattegno (1911-88), creator of the "subordination of teaching to learning," and perceived that he could never hope to instruct others without first understanding his own process of learning. This book, originally published in 1977 and now substantially revised, represents the results of his attempt to study himself and apply his findings to practical situations, especially with reluctant and discouraged writers of all ages.

He has published widely in academic journals and magazines and is the co-author, with Peter Miller, of Becoming a Writer (1986). He and Professor Miller were also co-editors of the Journal of Basic Writing, a peer-reviewed journal published by CUNY. Since 1990, much of his focus has been on the application of computer technology to writing in the spirit of "the subordination of teaching to learning," first in a computer-assisted classroom and subsequently on the internet.

He is one of the founders of the Bronx Charter School for Better Learning, a public primary school in New York dedicated to "the subordination of teaching to learning" that has demonstrated, over a fifteen-year period, that every child can become, in Ted Swartz's words, "a responsible and independent learner with a sustained love of learning."

JUST WRITING

JUST WRITING

Exercises to improve your writing

BILL BERNHARDT

Duo Flumina

First published in the United States of America
by Teachers & Writers in 1977
Copyright © 1977 by Bill Bernhardt

This new edition published by Duo Flumina Ltd
112 Warner Road, London SE5 9HQ, England in 2019
www.duoflumina.com
ISBN: 978-0-9568755-2-5

All rights reserved. No part of this book may be reprinted or reproduced or utilized in any form or by any electronic, mechanical, or other means, now known or hereafter invented, including photocopying and recording, or in any information storage or retrieval system, without permission in writing from the publisher.

I can't write today because I'm tired

I can't write today because I don't want to

I can't write today because I have nothing to write about

I can't write today because I'm sick of writing

I can't write today because my writing hand is tired

I can't write today because I was looking at pictures

I can't write today because my mind is on other things

I can't write today because my pen is running out of ink

I can't write today because it is thursday

I can't write today because I'm hungry

I can't write today because it is cold in this room

I can't write today because I'm thirsty

I can't write today because I like just sitting here

I can't write today because I have written so much in the past that I need a day off

I can't write today because my feet hurt

I can't write today because there's a bulb out in the room

I can't write today because I have no paper

I can't write today because I'm horny

I can't write today because I don't deserve the punishment

I can't write today because it's not sunny out

I can't write today because I'd rather be home asleep

I can't write today because I'd rather be home playing my guitar

I can't write today because I ran out of space on the paper

                                            Staten Island Community College Student

Foreward to the Original Edition

Most writing books—as difficult as they make the writing of essays appear—actually depict writing itself as much easier than it actually is. (What they make difficult is the paraphernalia *around or on top* of writing). How many texts have you seen that begin with instructions such as "limit your subject" or "make an outline" or "sharpen your thesis." These instructions suggest that ideas, or subject matter, are right there, ready to be narrowed or clarified or ordered. But an accurate description of what happens when a person sits down to write—especially a beginning writer—is that there are no ideas there. Instead of moving right into ordering and shaping, most writers begin inevitably with the "sit and stare fidgets" and the "bite your nails blanks."

Writing, especially when taught in the artificial setting of a course and a classroom, starts way back before structure. It starts in the hazy part of the brain where we mostly have hunches and intuitions. And almost nobody writes about how to get in contact with that material and how to then get it into verbal form so that someone else can profit from or enjoy or hear it. That's what I mean by most books not giving an accurate picture of how complex writing is. They make it seem too pat, too amendable to a form or container. For many, the form is the thing. Actually, writing is messy. It is unpredictable. It isn't linear in its making, though it has to be linear in its public presentation. It wobbles back and forth from sense to nonsense, from hint to statement. There's an awful lot of play that goes on in the writing process, play in the sense of "there's some play in the steering wheel." And very few composition texts allow that this is so.

All the more reason why I'm proud to write a foreword for Bill Bernhardt's book on "just writing." Bill has a very clear idea of how writing is connected to the rest of the human being, how it is actually a manifestation of the total human being. He isn't confused in thinking that the structure is the content or that writing must always occur in essay form. I like the way he startles readers and writers into thinking creatively, even if they aren't accustomed to thinking creatively. I like the way he shows that studying writing can also be about studying what you do—physically, emotionally, mentally—when you put pen to paper. I enjoy being shown how what I write is integrally connected to what I see, to what I experience, to what I imagine, to what I do. I respond with excitement to seeing writing as an activity of *life* instead of just an activity of a *course*.

I hope lots of people read this book. In fact, I wish that college freshmen all over the United States would use this text as a supplement to their regular writing text. Students who use Just Writing will understand the writing process, will discover the connection writing has to the rest of their activities. They will then be much more ready to move into more structured, formal areas of writing instruction.

And I hope everybody who would just like to enjoy the power of writing, the personal pleasure of putting pen to paper, will read the book. It might seem funny to think of recommending a book on writing as a response to hearing someone say something like, "Boy, you know I'm really in a rut. My life is boring." But Bill Bernhardt has so closely connected the act of writing to the act of living that I'd be happy to make such a recommendation. And I do.

Elizabeth Wooten Cowan
Possum Creek, Tennessee
July 1, 1977

Elizabeth Wooten Cowan was professor of English at Texas A & M, Director of English programs for the Modern Language Association, and coordinator of the Association of Departments of English.

Acknowledgments for the Original Edition

The personal essays which begin each chapter, the order of topics, and the phrasing of the exercises in this book are my own invention. I cannot claim anything else here as exclusively my own.

Many of the exercises are common knowledge in the sense that everyone who has ever made a careful study of writing has found them for himself or herself. Others are less widely known, although many of them might be duplicated in a number of sources. I cannot claim to have read all of the available sources, or always to remember where I first encountered this or that exercise. So I hope I may be forgiven for failing to credit others where credit is due.

I am, however, very conscious of my debts to Peter Elbow, James Moffett, Caleb Gattegno, and others who have also been inspired by the writings, seminars, and conversation of these men. Really, my debt to Dr. Gattegno is evident on every page. I only hope that my readers will be led back to his work by my contributions and refrain from judging his achievements by my mistakes and omissions.

Of all those who have also worked with Dr. Gattegno and helped me, I feel the greatest debts to Leonard Allison, Dorothea Hinman, Rose Katz Ortiz, and Robert J. Perrault. It was Bob Perrault, in fact, who first made me aware of Dr. Gattegno. Without his friendship and counsel during the past twenty-one years I could never have been able to write this book.

I must also thank my many students, in particular those who allowed me to include their work in this book, as well as my colleagues at The College of Staten Island.

It would have been impossible for me to begin or finish my writing of this book without the constant love and support of Elizabeth Farber, my wife. She convinced me that I was ready to do it and helped me every step of the way.

This book could never have reached its present state without a massive effort by Teachers & Writers Collaborative. I especially want to thank Miguel Ortiz, Steve Schrader, and Adalberto Ortiz.

Preface to the Revised Edition

This book was originally published in 1977, just a few years before "word processing" became the default tool for writing, followed by many other computer-based technologies. Readers will notice, therefore, that I refer more often to pens and pencils than to keyboards or other devices for creating/manipulating text. I deliberately chose not to update those references to traditional writing instruments. Readers can decide for themselves to what extent what is proposed in this book can be applied to their own preferred writing tools, some of which may be still in the trial stage as I write this sentence! For example, I recently surveyed a commercial catalogue displaying more than 20 new types of wireless styli for writing on a variety of hand-held devices. I could also have found the hardware and software that enable a similar set of speech-to-text dictation tools.

One reason for neglecting what has recently been invented to improve on pencils and pens is that so many self-styled practical tools for writing are ephemeral. Older readers will recall how Microsoft Word, backed by a very powerful commercial enterprise, was able to clear many superior competing products from the field. I also feel some nostalgia for tablet PCs from the early 2000s that supported intuitive free form annotation more successfully than any computer platform currently available in 2017. But there is a more important reason not to stress technology at the expense of other aspects of writing: because it can easily detract from the fact that written expression is a human activity for which technology plays only a minor supporting role. We do students a disservice if we persuade them otherwise.

Note on Encoding in Non-Alphabetic Writing Systems:
When I wrote the first edition of this book, I was largely unaware of the differences in the challenges of encoding (transcribing) English and those of a non-alphabetic "character" system as used for Chinese, for example. Therefore,

some of the experiments detailed in this book may need to be modified if the reader's aim is to understand the specific somatic and visual demands of encoding in non-alphabetic writing systems.

Acknowledgments for the Revised Edition

Just Writing remained in print for over 25 years thanks to the support of Teachers and Writers Collaborative. Since then, many readers and friends have urged me to re-publish it on paper or on the internet, but I always hesitated. I was finally moved to act when Roslyn Young and Piers Messum, two colleagues and friends from the world-wide community of Caleb Gattegno's students, offered to become the publishers. Whatever improvements may be evident in this revised edition are due to their encouragement. The faults and limitations remain my own.

Great thanks are due to Hanna Field for her delightful re-imagining of the illustrations for this book.

Table of Contents

What This Book Is About, Who It Is For, How It Is Organized 1

Section I – What Writing Is 3
    What "Knowing How to Write" Means 4
    Some Obvious Truths about Writing 7

Section II – Exercises and Activities for Becoming a Writer 13
    Back to Basics 14
    A Short Course in Just Writing 22
    Practical Exercises for Rapid Growth in Writing 38
    Transforming What One Writes 46
    Mastering the Mechanics of Writing 53
    Testing Oneself as a Writer 66

Section III – Studies for the Enhancement of Writing 71
    Starting Points for Exploring the Universe of Writing 72
    The Spirit of English 82
    Studying Words 104

Section IV – Research Activities for Teachers of Writing 121
    Investigating the Invisible Parts of Writing 122
    Studying Writers in the Classroom 133

What This Book Is About, Who It Is For, How It Is Organized

The subject of this book is *writing*—what it is; how to do it; what one needs to know to teach others how to write.

Countless books have already been written on this subject. Most of them are intended for a particular, specialized audience, such as college students, teachers of college composition, primary school children, aspiring professional authors, literary scholars, linguists, and so on. In addition, most of the existing texts are either narrowly practical or broadly theoretical, seldom both together.

My experience as a student, teacher, and teacher of teachers has shown me that the study of writing isn't helped by such fragmentation. An already mysterious subject is only further confused when we assume that the process of writing is essentially different when the person who learns is twenty-six instead of six or when we assume that only students (or "remedial" students) have "problems" learning what writing is and how to do it.

The truth is that writing is a "problem" for most people in our society, whatever their age, educational level, or profession. Most people who make their living teaching writing are not different from anyone else in this respect—they find it a very hard chore and they avoid doing it whenever possible.

Starting from the fact that most people are troubled about writing, I set out to create a text addressed to the needs of *anyone* who is dissatisfied with his or her understanding of writing, whether as a learner or a teacher or both. I assume, however, that most readers will be teachers and I have organized the sequence of topics in a way they may find particularly beneficial.

Before saying something about the organization of this book, I need to mention another principle which guided me in writing it. I know from my own experience that it is difficult to gain new knowledge and awareness through reading because written texts provide words, not experience. With this in mind, I have tried, whenever possible, to present what I have to say in the form of practical exercises and experiments. These the reader may use to generate experience which will provide him or her with the evidence for making an independent judgement. From speaking to people who have seen my work in manuscript, I know that this mode of presentation makes the book slow and difficult reading. But I don't see how I could have done otherwise since my purpose is to provide the essential tools for understanding writing, not to argue for my own ideas and opinions. I hope that my readers will find that the time and effort required to perform the exercises is justified; that they acquire greater clarity and certainty about writing through engaging with the questions I have provided; that they use this book to make new discoveries for themselves.

The book is divided into several sections. The first, consisting of two chapters of primary interest to teachers, provides a general orientation to my approach. These chapters are expository in nature and contain no exercises. The second section is composed primarily of exercises and is recommended as the proper starting place for all readers who wish to become more fluent and more confident writers. The third section contains more advanced exercises and experiments both in writing and the linguistic awarenesses that enhance writing skill. The last section is devoted to the pursuit of questions of concern to those teaching speech and writing—especially those whose work puts them in contact with challenging students.

How To Read This Book

The introduction to each chapter can be read in the usual way one reads anything—to see if the author's words make sense and if one can agree on the basis of past experience and knowledge.

But the exercises and activities have to be read in another way. They are not statements of what the author thinks. They are invitations to DO something, NOW, and then to reflect on the experience you had while doing it.

The primary purpose of this book is to provide experiences which you can think about while they are still fresh. But this can only happen with the reader's cooperation.

If you insist on reading the exercises in the usual way, and at your usual speed, you will miss an opportunity to do something different for a change.

The first page of exercises in each chapter was designed to be done first, in the order given. The rest can be done in any order desired. There's no need to finish all of one chapter before starting another.

Start with an exercise or two and see whether you get something from it—not words but an experience. If you do, why not read others slowly and carefully? There's no hurry. This isn't a treatise to be read all at once, but a workbook. A workbook which provides experience. Maybe one or two experiences is enough for one day.

Section I: What Writing Is

For the most part, this book contains things you can *do*, working alone or with other people, to study writing for yourself. It is composed mainly of activities, exercises, and experiments rather than lectures or lessons.

This first portion of the book is different from the rest in that it is more theoretical than practical. It is intended for people who want to be told what the author thinks and what he has in mind before considering any of the exercises.

The supporting evidence of what is said in this section can be found by working through the rest of the book. If what is asserted here seems unclear or unconvincing, the reader may wish to suspend his or her judgement until after reading other parts of the book.

What "Knowing How to Write" Means

I've been a teacher of writing for more than a dozen years. For most of that time I was sure I knew how to tell if someone could write or not. It was easy. The person would show me something he or she had composed, and I would read it over to myself. If what was on the paper made sense and was expressed in halfway decent English, I concluded that the author knew how to write. If it wasn't, he or she didn't.

Several years ago something happened to shake my confidence in this simple test of writing ability. When I started watching my students as they were writing and asking them questions about their experience as writers, I made a discovery: some of the people I had come to think of as my "best" writers went through agonies each time they had to pick up a pencil. They had to work through draft after draft in order to achieve results which they could live with. Finally, they confessed that in spite of their apparent "success" (teachers had *always* praised their work), they never felt inwardly convinced that they knew how to write. Some of my weaker students, on the other hand, seemed to enjoy writing even if the results were less than impressive.

Making these observations set me to thinking. I asked myself whether it made sense to assume that people knew "how to write" if they went through hell each time they had to do it. Was it possible that many of my students were somehow managing to "get writing done" even though they didn't really know "how"?

I quickly saw that there were many more questions I had to ask myself: When does a person know "how"? Is it when he or she can produce acceptable work, no matter how long it takes and no matter how much effort and determination it requires? Or is "knowing how" a question of inner control and efficiency? Does a person know "how" when he or she knows what has to be done, mentally, in order to overcome inhibitions, to find something to say, and to direct the hand to transmit it onto a page? In other words, is "knowing how" judged by outward results or an internal functioning sense of what to do?

During most of my time as a teacher, I was interested only in the quality of what my students produced. Whether it took five minutes or five hours to complete an assignment didn't concern me. The important question was always "how good is the *paper*?" Now I have come to see that this way of thinking is more appropriate to literary criticism than to teaching writing. If I am involved in teaching people how to write I have to care not only about "the paper" but also about the *person* who composed it. I need to know if that person is using himself in a productive way.

"Using oneself productively" is shorthand for a number of things. It means, above all, getting a fair return for the energy and time invested in an activity. One can say "I am using myself productively in writing" only if energy is mobilized

Section I: What Writing Is

for doing the things that actually produce writing rather than squandered in anxieties and distractions. Another test is whether the time spent is consumed by "doing" or only by "trying." More specifically, it means focusing on what one wants to say instead of worrying about whether what comes out is "good," or if it will please the teacher, or if it follows the rules learned in school. Further, "using oneself productively" includes accepting the ideas and images and words that come to mind, committing them to paper while they are still vivid, and leaving spelling, neatness, and editing until later—when one has already generated something to work with. And it includes moving the pencil fast enough to catch the words before they are forgotten, or replaced by new ones. And it includes listening to the sentences to make sure that they "sound like English" as well as looking to see that all of the words in the sentence reach the page, not just some of them. Finally, "using oneself productively" means doing all of these things with sufficient facility that the act of writing becomes gradually more "automatic" (the way speaking is) and one need never dread picking up a pencil.

From talking to lots of people who have finished their formal education, including many teachers and professional writers, I've gathered that few "literate" individuals use themselves productively. Nor do they ever lose their dread and fear of writing. If they have the time, and can summon up the determination to stick with it, they can struggle to produce the essay, or letter, or poem they set out to write. But after years of practice in writing, and after producing many satisfactory (maybe even "good") results, they still feel traumatized by this activity. However much they are praised or congratulated by others, furthermore, they still lack the functional know-how they need to be at peace with writing.[1]

It is essential for anyone who wants to study writing—as a student or a teacher—to know "how to write" in this functional sense. No body of knowledge "about" writing can possibly substitute for direct, first-person experience of what it means to function as a facile writer. To this extent, the study of writing is the *same* for students (of any age), teachers, and teachers of teachers. But there is an additional sense of "how to write" that is required of teachers and not of students.

People who simply want to function as writers know that they have "succeeded" from the feedback the activity itself provides. As soon as they have acquired some facility (within the limits of their own vocabulary) and are no longer threatened by the activity of writing, all that is necessary and sufficient for accelerated progress has been gained—only practice will be needed in order to reach higher levels of performance. For people who want to teach writing, however, this feedback is necessary but not sufficient. Teachers must also acquire

---

1 Practical approaches for attaining functional know-how are provided in the second section of this book.

an awareness—as precise as possible—of what they have done with themselves to reach the threshold of writing at will.

Many teachers who are good writers themselves imagine that their memories will guide them when they come to instruct students. They recall a sequence of exercises, or "steps," which accompanied their first fruitful experience of writing and attempt to replicate them in the classroom. More often than not, their students respond with the same proportion of success and failure as in any class where "bright ideas" are the order of the day.

It is difficult to answer the question of how one learned to write through memory. In the first place, memory deceives us. What comes back through the selective process of recall is not the event itself but anecdotes, images, and interpretations. Secondly, one's process of recollection may be colored and distorted by intellectual prejudices and beliefs. Finally, if one passed through the experience without perceiving any but the most superficial aspects, even the most faithful memory will be unhelpful.

Most of us, when we learned to write, were concerned with achieving certain immediate, practical results, not with observing our own inner processes. For this reason, what we remember is of scant use to us when we become teachers. It is necessary, therefore, for the person who wants to teach writing to make a new study of the process, uncontaminated by memory.

The basis for deliberate teaching of others is learning how to observe what one does within oneself *here and now* to sustain one's facility in writing. Such self-study does not come easily. Some entry into it is provided in the following chapter and in the concluding section of this book. For the present it is sufficient to say this: To function as a writer requires doing the right things within oneself, and there is no requirement to be articulate about what they are. To be a conscious, deliberate teacher, however, requires a precise and articulate understanding of what the functioning "know-how" entails.

Some Obvious Truths about Writing

I've always been impressed by detective stories. Although I read them mostly for entertainment, I have learned a valuable lesson from them—that the "obvious" is not what usually gets noticed first. Sherlock Holmes said, "I have trained myself to see what others overlook," and I know that this is something that I need to be constantly reminded to do. For most of the time I "overlook" what is right under my nose in order to invent fanciful theories and chase exotic clues to the mysteries in my life. I know that others behave in the same way. So perhaps I don't need to apologize for beginning with some common-sense observations about writing that others have considered too "obvious" to mention.

Just because something is "obvious" is no guarantee that its significance can be absorbed at once. That's obvious. For this reason, I consider most of the points listed below worthy of careful consideration. Perhaps I only echoed the words? Can I devise an experiment or test to see whether it is really true? How could I make practical use of this in my own learning and teaching?

There are, first of all, certain common-sense observations one can make about writing that apply equally to most other activities people engage in:

It is a human activity.

We need complex rather than simple models for looking at things that people do, for people are complicated. In particular, we need to remember that our actions have to be looked at from both outside and inside. What shows on the outside is "behavior." But we all know that there is so much inside that doesn't show on the surface: movements of energy, intentions, images, emotions, consciousness, and so on. All of these things are part of our experience as writers.

It is a voluntary activity.

The muscles that direct our fingers to push the pen or depress the typewriter keys are controlled by our will. And it is through the exercise of our will that we decide to pursue this topic rather than that one, to enhance this image and drop that one, to choose this word rather than that one, or to make any outward expression of our thoughts at all. Since no one else is inside making our fingers move, only the writer can cause writing to happen.

It is an internal process.

The movement of certain limbs, the appearance of certain tracings on a piece of paper signal that writing is happening. But the process of which those outward appearances are only the final outcome takes place internally and invisibly. This process has many components: the inhibitions a person feels and may or may not overcome; the awareness that one has something to say though the words for it may or may not come; the triggering of words to fit one's meaning; the many changes and revisions that intervene between the moment when one first grasps some words and the time when one begins to prepare oneself somatically for the physical exertion of transcription.

Its internal process is only accessible through consciousness of oneself.

What happens inside at the moment of writing is a total mystery from outside. To most people, it is a blur, a partial mystery, from inside. If they have "trouble," they do not know where the "block" is located, only that it exists. But through conscious exploration of oneself much of the mystery can be unveiled. We can discover whether our block lies in the force of inhibitions, or in neglect of mental imagery as a trigger of language, or in inability to hold words long enough for their transcription, or any one of many possible causes. Without the lightings of consciousness, however,

none of these "problems" can be illuminated.

It is hierarchical in time.

We can't learn everything at once. Some things must come before others—such as the fact that we speak before we write, and we scribble before we make "letters." But it is easy for us to become confused about the hierarchical sequence and to substitute tidy schemas for what actually occurs—as when we assume that a descriptive knowledge of grammar must precede practice in free composition or that one literary genre is intrinsically more "advanced" than other.

The essential preparation takes place outside school.

No one "teaches" us to speak, to generate ideas, to evoke images, to want to express ourselves. Nor do we need instruction in order to learn how to tell lies, to make rationalizations, to create narratives, rhymes, or to engage in any number of expressive modes. All of these abilities are normally developed in early childhood by interaction with the environment. They continue to be practiced in dreams and inner speech (if not elsewhere) throughout life. So whatever the educational background or "level" of any learner, he or she comes to the formal study of writing with a rich endowment.

What others tell us doesn't help much.

Words are arbitrary noises without inherent meaning, so verbal explanations have limited utility except when the listener has definite experiences to bring to what is said. In any event, talking "about" an activity can only convey vicarious experience. It cannot convey the experience itself. Thus the basis for learning writing is writing, plunging into the activity rather than receiving advice and explanations.

The most difficult phase is getting started.

Most courses and methods stress editorial revision and proofreading skills. But the majority of people have trouble at a much earlier stage. Their difficulties in composing are compounded, furthermore, by the fact that they "edit out" most of their thoughts and words before anything reaches the page. What does manage to be set down seems in need of heavy editing because of the process by which it was put there—in disconnected fits, with lapses of consciousness between words and in between sentences.

The most potent interference is our desire for immediate perfection.

Wanting to be perfect at once makes it difficult to start and, once begun, to make any further progress. In order to be truly engaged in the activity of writing the inevitability of mistakes and errors must be acknowledged.

There are, secondly, certain observations one can make about writing that this activity shares with speaking:

It is overwhelmingly "synthetic" rather than "analytic."

Much is left hazy when writing is described in terms of inspiration or intuition, but such expressions are closer to the actuality of composing than attempts to approach it in terms of discrete skills such as vocabulary, sentence structure, paragraph organization, etc. Both writing and speaking demand that one use all of oneself at once, not simply one faculty at a time.

It requires specific somatic awarenesses.

To the extent that one can identify discrete components of the writing process, it is possible to discriminate between sensitivities developed in the centers of hearing and voice production and sensitivities located in the muscles that make the transcription. Part of learning to write is a matter of experiencing the sounds in the throat and mouth, testing them against the ear, and feeling the shapes of the words in the arms and fingers. In this respect, writing is an athletic activity.

It requires a training of one's ears and voice.

The voice is our tool for synthesizing all of the many components that comprise language (sounds and the sequence of sounds; words and the silences between words; words and the "tune" of the language onto which they fit). The ear is our tool for gauging when the language we generate sounds both correct and right.

Technically considered, it is a system of arbitrary signs.

Speech is a system of sounds and silence; writing of notations and spaces. In either case, the selection of signs is arbitrary. Neither sounds nor notations have any meaning of their own. We simply have to accept what the inventors of these complementary systems of signs have passed onto us.

It is, by construction, vague and imprecise.

Language, whether oral or written, is shared by everyone who uses it. Our own experience, on the other hand, is unique and individual. Because language has to serve everyone as a common carrier, it is never perfectly adjusted to the specific needs of a single individual user. We can never find an exact expression of our unique meaning, only an approximation which is compatible with what is inside us.

The first threshold is facility.

In both speaking and writing, a high frequency of errors can be tolerated—especially in a permissive language such as English. We do not judge whether a person speaks or writes on the basis of frequency or absence of errors, but on the basis of his or her ability to say something spontaneously and easily.

It exists for expression.

When we speak or write, we can know what we intend to say. But we cannot know whether our message is actually carried by the words because that depends on someone else—our listener or reader. The ideal of language may be communication, but the reality is expression.

There are, finally, certain observations one can make about writing that are unique to this activity (or shared only with reading).

It is dependent on speech.

Writing can be considered a visually coded approximation of oral speech. The key term here is "approximation," for writing isolates one component—words—and abstracts it from the whole body of phenomena that makes speech a carrier of meaning—that is, silence, stress, melody, intonation, speed of utterance, phrasing, etc. In fact, writing deliberately distorts speech through the convention of placing equal spaces between words. Because the written form of the language is so impoverished by comparison to oral speech, the demands of expression in this medium are more stringent. Further, many of the problems learners encounter in writing result when they are expected to function with facility using versions of the language ("standard English," "essay English") that they do not speak, or speak only with difficulty.

Its system of signs contains many inconsistencies and much untidiness.

This observation is particularly true of English, but it is a characteristic of all languages that the correlation between the system of sound-signs and the system of visual-signs is inexact. In fact, there are actually two systems of visual coding—one for the verbal component of the language (spelling) and another for the nonverbal, sonic elements (punctuation). Neither is fully consistent although the second is particularly imprecise and inadequate.

It presents certain mechanical problems.

The voice is quick and the hand is slow. Even the most hesitant speaker can compose more rapidly, and with greater economy of effort, than the practiced writer can transcribe. Consequently, there is always a lapse in time between finding words and setting them down on paper. Each writer must develop special techniques for "holding" all the words of an utterance until such time as the hand can transcribe them. It is perhaps inevitable that the demands of composition and transcription should conflict, often with unfortunate consequences for one or the other. For this reason, many people deliberately choose to separate the two operations: composing with the aid of a recording device and transcribing their expression at some later time.

It confers permanence.

Oral speech is, by nature, ephemeral. Although it permits almost instantaneous revision and expansion—which writing does not allow—it is unsuited to preservation and successive revisions over an extended period of time. Writing, on the other hand, is a medium that can be easily frozen in time and transmitted over space. For these reasons, it is eminently suited to the expression of our second thoughts and considered statements. Viewed from this perspective, writing easily becomes synonymous with "rewriting."

Section II:
Exercises and Activities for Becoming a Writer

This portion of the book contains a number of chapters, each one consisting of a brief introduction followed by several pages of suggestions for things to do. Because this a "workbook" and not a treatise, you can only get out of it what you put into doing the exercises and finding answers to the questions—your own answers, not the author's.

The practical exercises and activities contained in this section have proven useful to learners of all ages and on all "levels." Many more could have been added to make this section longer. The choice of so few is deliberate. I have included only those exercises that are fundamental, that make learners aware of the demands of writing in all circumstances. What is offered is required of every writer, whether he or she is primarily interested in prose or poetry, "creative" or discursive writing.

The chapters in this section are placed in a certain order deliberately. The most important and fundamental come first; the rest follow in a descending order of importance.

Just Writing

Back to Basics

Anyone who comes to study writing expects to begin with what are called "the fundamentals," the necessary "first steps," the "foundations," or "the basics." Since one thing *has* to come before another, because it's impossible to learn everything at once, we want to start with "essentials"—those learnings that form the basis for everything that follows. The experts, however, have never been able to agree about what "the basics" of writing are. For this reason, every book on composition, and just about every teacher, offers a different interpretation of "the basics." One expert is convinced that an understanding of linguistics is crucial whereas another insists on classical rhetoric; a third believes in traditional grammar while a fourth has still another preference. It would take a lifetime to become familiar with all the different interpretations which have been offered for "the basics."

It is quite unnecessary to get drawn into this debate. If this phrase—"the basics"—means anything, it must refer to some body of skills (or we can call them abilities, or learnings, or awarenesses) that can be demonstrated to be fundamental and indispensable for *all* people who learn to write. Clearly, none of the various candidates for this title that have been proposed could possibly qualify since (a) plenty of people manage quite well without exposure to them and (b) plenty of people manage very poorly in spite of having been exposed to them. In other words, neither traditional grammar, nor transformational grammar, nor classical rhetoric, nor sentence combining, nor free writing, nor any other so-called basic exercise has proven to be absolutely necessary for everyone learning to write.

Perhaps teachers and theorists go off the track because they try to approach writing as an activity that can actually be taught "from the beginning." The truth is that no human functioning is fully isolated and self-contained. They are all located in time. That is, whatever we learn at any given moment is always supported by a base of earlier learnings. As the old proverb says, "You can't walk before you can crawl."

If we want to locate the base upon which the skills of writing are necessarily built, we have to look backwards in time—to abilities and powers of ourselves that are not generally an acknowledged part of the process of learning to write. For example, without having prepared our selves to function as both scanning and focusing instruments we could never make sense of the technical demands of writing. And without some facility in talking to ourselves (not necessarily to others) how could we ever compose silently on paper?

It is easy to come up with a vast catalogue of prior learnings that might in some way contribute to learning to write. For example: scribbling, storytelling, daydreaming, complaining, impersonating, vocabulary building, discriminating shapes, discriminating sounds, remembering, etc. The important question, however, is which items on such a list are necessary and indispensable? All of them may be useful, but which are the ones we cannot do without if we want to acquire the skill of writing?

Specialists in the teaching of children—particularly children with apparent "learning disabilities" —have given themselves to one aspect of this question. They have defined, with some precision, certain perceptual and manual skills that are basic to writing. But far less attention has been given to defining those abilities that, while essential, are nontechnical in nature. There are many specialists in hand-writing, few in composing.

As it happens, the great majority of people (of any age) have their greatest difficulty with the non-technical aspects of writing. They learn to master legibility and spelling, but they never become very facile in having something to say and getting it down on paper. Clearly, "the basics" that most of us need further exposure to are in the area of speech rather than the purely formal conventions of writing.

It is a truism that people learn to speak their native language before they learn to write it. Everyone assumes that speech is somehow basic to writing. Still, it is equally obvious that many "verbal" people remain illiterate or, if they learn to write, never attain facility. So while we must say that speech is necessary for writing, we cannot say that it is sufficient.

My own study of talking and writing has shown me that there are certain abilities that, while not always very important in social uses of spoken speech, are essential to writing. And it is these skills that most people who have "problems" with written composition have failed to practice adequately. These are "the basics" of speech upon which writing depends:

> **Talking to oneself.** This is a process by which words (and sentences and paragraphs) are generated, improved, and prepared for transcription on a page.
>
> **Listening to oneself.** This is the tool by which utterances are "checked" to make certain that they make sense, sound "right," and contain enough words to convey, adequately, what one has in mind.
>
> **Holding the words of an utterance.** This is the ability that permits us to make sure that what we transcribe is not an approximation but a full and faithful rendering of whatever we have to say. We need to practice this because our voice works so much faster in composing than our hand in transcribing.

Once I discovered that those skills formed the basis for writing, I began to notice something about myself I had never observed before. I recognized that since my early childhood I had been engaged in verbal dialogues within myself, dialogues in which I kept my talking and listening skills alive through constant practice. Whether I was daydreaming or engaged in conversation, I was busy talking and listening to myself, perpetually generating statements and working to improve them. "Holding," however, was something I did *not* practice spontaneously. These observations showed me why my "problem" in writing has always been grammar rather than content. Since I had prepared myself to generate and improve statements in my inner speech, I was seldom at a loss for words. When I came to transcribe my inventions, on the other hand, I was not adequately prepared to hold all of the words long enough for my pencil to record them. In fact, I often left out words and parts of words (endings especially) with the result that my sentences appeared ungrammatical.

The following pages contain practical exercises that can enable a person to gain facility in "the basics" that speech contributes to writing. Although these exercises may seem unfamiliar at first to some readers, they will be quickly picked up—for each of us has been engaged in similar activities as babies learning our language for the first time. To this extent, what is proposed is not a new way of using oneself but a process of renewal.

I want to stress that these exercises *must* be done "in one's head" or "in the air" and not on paper. The succeeding chapter will contain exercises for facilitating the transfer of these "basic skills" from speech to writing.

Basics 1

Wherever you are at *this* particular moment, begin muttering to yourself. It doesn't matter what you mutter about, the essential thing is to translate whatever images, feelings, or thoughts you have in your mind at this moment into words … and to say them.

If what you have in your mind at this moment is a sense that you don't have anything to mutter about, then mutter about having nothing to mutter about.

If you are alone, speak aloud and make the words come out. If you are with other people, do your muttering inside, or with your lips moving slightly.

Repeat this exercise as often as possible until words come easily at any time, and until you can mutter silently or out loud with equal facility.

❊ ❊ ❊

When you are doing something you do every day—such as driving to work, washing dishes, downloading an app, etc.—provide a "play-by-play" description of what is happening as it happens.

Some of your play-by-play can be from your own point of view ("Now I'm …") and some from outside ("Now she's …").

Practice until you can do this at will, anytime, anywhere. And until you can do it aloud; silently, but with your lips moving; completely "inside."

Basics 2

Look around you and force yourself to keep on talking in a whisper about whatever you see for a minute or more without stopping. It doesn't matter if what you say is trivial or repetitive—the important thing is to keep your whispered monologue going.

Even though you are speaking in a whisper, make sure that the noise which comes out sounds like English—that is, put plenty of expression into it.

Practice frequently until you can do this anytime, anywhere, at will.

❊ ❊ ❊

Repeat the exercise above with the following variations:

Do the talking in your head without making a sound. (It's okay if your lips move just as long as no sound comes out.)

Repeat each sentence at least twice so that you can be certain that your inner voice speaks clearly and distinctly and your inner hearing is acute.

Practice frequently until you feel confident that the voice you use in these silent monologues is as fluent and expressive as the voice you use for speaking to other people, and until you know that your hearing of this silent voice is as sensitive as when listening to others.

Basics 3

Each of the problems given below requires that you do two things. First, you must talk (either out loud or in your head) with as much force and expression as possible. If it helps to gesture with your hand or move your whole body while you talk, do it! Second, you must listen to yourself and stop to make improvements whenever you hear anything that doesn't sound right or could be said better another way.

Practice speaking and listening to yourself, and make improvements as often as possible so that it becomes second nature.

(1) What you might say to someone who insulted your mother.

(2) A joke that builds up, slowly, to a good punch line.

(3) An explanation of something you know about which most people don't know—a practical skill, a scientific explanation, etc.

(4) Why you like or dislike a certain person whom you know.

***

Practice speaking and listening to yourself, and make improvements whenever situations such as the following provide you with opportunities:

You know you are going to be interviewed or asked questions and you are able to rehearse your answers in advance.

You are dissatisfied with what you said in a conversation with someone else and can now work on preparing a more adequate statement of whatever you had in mind.

Due to circumstances beyond your control, you weren't able to speak your mind in a certain social situation, but you can now practice what it would have been appropriate to say.

Hearing someone else speak in public, you know that you could prepare a better presentation of the same ideas or position.

Section II: Becoming a Writer

Basics 4

Wherever you are at this moment, look around you and say what you see in answer to each of the following questions:

What "stands out"?

Is there anything here that has special meaning or significance for me?

Is there anything here that reminds me of something else?

What can I notice only if I look very carefully?

Is there anything here I have a strong opinion about?

What seems hard to understand or brings questions into my mind?

Practice talking to yourself in this way whenever possible. Notice whether focusing your sight in response to such questions helps you find more to say than if you just "say what you see" without asking questions.

* * *

Observe a person, a picture, a piece of furniture, etc., and ask yourself at least ten intelligent questions about him/her/it.

Practice asking such questions and talking to yourself about how you might either answer them or go about finding the answers. Notice whether starting with questions helps you find something to talk about and keep talking.

* * *

Make an image in your mind of a person you know. Ask yourself questions about this person until you have remembered (or invented) enough detailed information to tell a story about him or her.

Practice this exercise frequently and notice whether making images helps you to ask questions. Notice also whether asking questions helps you evoke more images and/or more vivid images.

Continue practicing this exercise until you are able to make up stories about anyone you can picture in your mind—whether real or imaginary.

Basics 5

Experiment to see what is the longest sentence you can say to yourself (at normal speed) and repeat *exactly*, without changing or omitting a single word.

(If you have difficulty making sure that you are doing this correctly, count off the number of words—or phrases—on your fingers or a string of beads when you speak the first time. Then check your "repeat" to see if it contains the identical number of items. Or you can ask someone else to do the counting and tell you the *numbers* of the items in the sequence that have been omitted or changed.)

Practice this exercise, focusing on recovery of the missing items, until you can do it easily with a 30-word sentence.

* * *

Practice repeating a long sentence, deliberately adding or inserting one more word each time until you are holding a 50-word sentence.

* * *

Practice repeating a long sentence, deliberately substituting one new word each time without changing the rest. Continue making substitutions until your sentence contains none of its original words. (You don't have to change little words such as *and, of, for*, etc. unless you want to.)

* * *

Starting with a long sentence which begins with "I," change the "I" to "She" or "He" and repeat the original, making only those additional alterations that are necessary to preserve sense.

Notice the words that have to be changed or replaced in order to preserve sense. Where do they come in the sentence? Where do changes most often occur in the words—at the beginning or the end?

* * *

Starting with a sentence that describes something which happened at some time in the past, change it into a sentence describing something which is happening *now*—at this moment—but with as few changes as possible.

Notice the words that have to be changed to make this transformation of the original sentence. Where do they come in the sentence? How much of the word is changed?

Basics 6

Listen to various people who have distinctive personal styles of speech (preachers, politicians, TV personalities or dramatic characters, people who speak English as a second language, etc.). Try, when you are alone, to capture their ways of talking.

Practice until you are satisfied with some of your impersonations.

***

Choose someone whose way of talking impresses you and try, when you are alone, to impersonate him or her. See if you can not only sound like the person in terms of accent and melody but also use his or her distinctive vocabulary and turns of phrase.

Practice until you can slip in and out of this impersonation at will. Notice also whether you can use any of this person's verbal habits to enrich your own speech.

***

Practice talking to yourself in each of the following roles:

(1) A parent instructing children

(2) A child "talking back" to a parent

(3) A salesperson "pushing" a product or service

(4) A lover expressing his or her love

(5) A philosopher wondering about the meaning of life

(6) Someone who gives scientific explanations for everything

(7) Someone who always speaks in proverbs and sayings

(8) Someone who uses big words whenever possible

(9) Someone who chooses each word carefully

(10) Someone who talks all the time

A Short Course in Just Writing

Knowing that I am an "English" teacher, people often ask me, "Is there a place where I can go to study writing?" When this first started happening to me, about ten years ago, I used to reply by listing and describing the various graduate writing programs I knew about, and I was surprised to find how uninterested they were in what I had to say about Iowa, Stanford, or wherever. "No," someone would say, "That's not what I mean. I don't want to be a *creative writer*; I just want to learn to write. You know, just writing."

Once, only once, I answered the question by suggesting a course in English Composition, which I was teaching at the time. "Oh Christ!" my friend shouted, "Not another course in *English*. I don't want to study topic sentences, or compare and contrast the probable causes of the French Revolution. I just want to learn to write. You know, just writing."

Since then I have become aware that there is some place you can go and study almost every imaginable *kind* of writing whether it be radio scripts, directions for assembling stereo kits, advertising copy, concrete poetry, pornography, recipes for teen-age cooks, or whatever you like. But there is no place that offers instruction in "just writing."

I have to admit that it took me a long while to realize that "just writing" wasn't any empty phrase. It really meant something to the people who used it. What they meant was that they had studied verbs and adverbs, and sentences, and paragraphs, and essays, and creative writing, but they still couldn't sit down, pick up a pencil, and start writing without an incredible effort. Some of them had done well in school and some poorly; some had managed to grind out a Ph.D. dissertation, and some couldn't seem to cover half a page; but they all shared the same sense of blankness and dread when the word "writing" was mentioned.

I was astonished to discover that there was often so little difference between those who had been "good in English" and those who had failed. I was even more surprised when I found out that many of my fellow teachers were no less traumatized by writing than their students! It seemed that practically everybody I met feared and hated the activity of writing, whatever their personal history or level of education.

There had been a time when I felt the same way but it was so far in the past that I really couldn't remember it clearly or reconstruct what I had done to overcome it. Still, I came to recognize that if I wanted to help others in meeting their writing blocks, I had to recover a sense of the thresholds I had needed to cross in learning to write. Making such a study of my own writing took me several years and is chronicled at various points throughout this book.

What I want to offer here is a practical approach to "just writing" demonstrating what the activity demands and the resources every one of us brings to it. The

Section II: Becoming a Writer

purpose of these exercises is not to make anyone a "good" writer, only to provide some instruments for increasing awareness of what writing is. Just writing.

Each of the pages in my "Short Course" is concerned with all of the things that a person must do with himself or herself in order to function as a writer. There is, however, a slightly different emphasis on each page. Page 1 should be done first. The other pages can be completed in any order. Or one can leave part of a page unfinished and turn to another page. Or course, the directions for the exercises can be either read by the person working on the course, or they can be delivered orally by someone else.

Just Writing 1

When you are with people with whom you feel comfortable, do you find that you have something to say? A lot?

* * *

Which comes first when you speak, knowing that you have something to say or the words? Test yourself to find out.

* * *

Once you start to speak, do you find that you have more to say as you keep talking? See what happens if you try to talk quickly, without stopping, for one full minute.

* * *

Make a short statement out loud.
Write down the same words you said.

> Are you sure that you wrote the same words? How can you tell? Can you make a much longer statement and write down the words accurately? (it doesn't matter if you misspell.)

* * *

Think of something else you could say but instead of speaking, write it down without speaking.

* * *

Can you think of something to say and write the words down as they come into your mind without taking the time to say them to yourself first?

Continue "talking with your pencil" for several minutes.

> Can you make your pencil move fast enough to get all of your words down? (Don't worry about spelling or punctuation.)

* * *

Experiment to see if you can think of what you want to say and write it down almost at the same moment.

* * *

Is there anything you could say that you can't also write down?

Section II: Becoming a Writer

(a) The writer, a student from a parochial school in Staten Island, N.Y., was shown a picture and asked to write whatever he wanted for 10 minutes.

A place in England a city which is very liveing spot a lot of people are leaving in this city and a lot of people visit this city to stay people come and visit this place to see thing old thing that they have not seen before thats what the city is being for old thing form the 1800s that people like to see.

(b) The same person was then asked to utter sentences to himself and then write them down exactly as he spoke them. This exercise took about five minutes.

My recorder broke down and I put it in the shop. So now I am waiting to get it out in a few days. I hope it doesen caused to much I don't have that much to pay. The arm of the recorder was the problem so it shouldn't caused that much.

Just Writing 2

Take a pencil and a piece of blank paper and write continuously for three minutes without removing your pencil from the paper. Use script rather than print and pay no attention to whether what you write makes sense or is spelled correctly. If you can't think of anything to say, just write down all the words you can think of. When you finish, turn the paper over without reading what you wrote.

Write for three more minutes on the reverse side of the paper, following the same directions.

Write for three more minutes on a second sheet of paper.

> Count how many words you wrote each time. Did your output increase the second and/or third time? Have you written more than you usually write in the same amount of time?
>
> Read what you wrote aloud and listen to yourself. Does it make sense? Does it sound like the English you speak?

* * *

Experiment to see if you can cover one complete page by writing continuously. As you write, catch yourself each time you start to think about spelling or about whether what you are writing is "good" or "bad."

> Read what you wrote aloud to someone else. Does it make sense to him or her?

* * *

When you write faster, do you find that you have more or less to say?

* * *

Does your writing make more sense when you write slowly? Does "making sense" have anything to do with the quality of your handwriting or spelling?

(a) First three-minute writing

I think that books should be given out free to all students in all education systems. I know that this sounds impossible because there's no money profit involved. But I do think students would benefit from this suggestion. Books that are used in college are very expensive and many students have to save for many weeks before they can buy all (61 words)

(b) Second three-minute writing

I could never imagine children growing up in a city. I myself have grown up in Staten Island, which had a country atmosphere when I grew up. I can remember playing in the field in the back of my house, running in the brook and getting very dirty. The most remarkable times I ever had were in woods. And around the brook. My older brother and his friends always built a swing over the brook in the summer. Climbing up the tree that contained the swing was no easy chore for a (92 words)

(c) Third three-minute writing

The worst job I ever had was in city. It was the best paying job I ever had but it was the most boring. I held the position of a cash clerk in the second largest stock firm, Bache and Company, Incorporated. The reason why this job was boring was because everything had to be done in the format A, B, C, & D. There was no intellectual knowledge needed for this job and it drove me up the wall. All day in work I had to day dream to keep myself from going crazy. The only pleasant thing I can remember was going to Chinatown to eat lunch. Another reason why I hated the was because (118 words)

Staten Island Community
College Student

Just Writing 3

Complete the following sentence by adding one word at the end:

    As they turned the corner they saw

Copy the completed sentence onto the top of a blank sheet of paper and continue by writing a second sentence that begins with the following word:

    Maybe

Add a third sentence to the story.

Add five more sentences to the story.

End the story.

> How much of the story was given to you and how much did you have to provide? Would anyone else write the same story you wrote?
>
> Could you see in your mind what was happening in the story? If so, was it like a photograph or a movie?
>
> Did you see the entire story at the beginning or did more come into your mind as you continued?
>
> Can you visualize the story all over again when you read the words you wrote?

✽ ✽ ✽

Close your eyes and picture in your mind a difficult or embarrassing situation you would not like to find yourself in.

Describe in writing what the situation is.

Write what you would say to get yourself out of that situation.

✽ ✽ ✽

Does making pictures in your mind help you think of things to say or write?

(a) *As they turned the corner they saw* a thief. *Maybe* he wasn't a thief but a man in a hurry. The man was running in the direction of the police station. When he got to the police station, he told the officer that there had been a robbery. The officer asked him who was robbed. The man replied "Me." The officer then took down all the information that he needed. He told the man to have a seat and try to relax and he would put a man on the case right away.

After three days of investigating a police officer found the criminal. He was arrested and sent to prison for fifteen years. The police found out that he was wanted for a number of other crimes. He found out the hard way that crime doesn't pay.

Staten Island Community
College Student

(b) *As they turned the corner they saw* Fred. *Maybe* Fred was going our way? So we asked him and he said he was on his way to the park. We told him we were too so we asked him if we too can come along. On the way we began to talk about the way we would like our future to turn out. Fred said that he would like to have a job that he would like and would have a lot of free time, to do what he wanted. My other friend said that he would be an accountant and make a lot of money. Fred said, what difference does it make if you make alot of money but never have enough free time to spend it. I said, I see both your points but I'd rather be in Fred's position. And then we got to the park and started to play basketball as we came here to do.

Staten Island Community
College Student

Just Writing 4

Close your eyes and sit silently for a moment. Imagine that someone you know well is talking to you.

Open your eyes and write down what they are saying. Try to capture the exact way they speak.

Can you hear the person's voice in what you wrote when you read your words aloud?

* * *

Imagine that you are the President of the United States making a speech on television.

Practice making your voice sound like the President's and speak for a few minutes in his style.

Write down the speech which you made. Later on, ask someone to read it aloud and listen to see if it sounds like the voice you had in mind.

* * *

Write a dialogue between two angry people.

* * *

Write any of the following that appeal to you:

    A letter to someone you love.

    A letter to someone you hate.

    A script for a TV commercial.

    A paragraph that will make someone you know angry.

    A paragraph that will make someone laugh.

"Letter to Someone You Love"

(Names are withheld at the writers' requests. All are former Staten Island Community College students.)

(a) To my Father—

I love you and I hate you. Sometimes I admire you so much that I really want to be just like you and sometimes I can't think of anyone in the world who disgusts me more than you do. You have more charm and appeal than any human person deserves but underneath your charm and appeal you are so selfish and rotten—how can you be so deceiving?

It's so strange, everything reminds me of you; shoes in a store window, a jacket that B—wears, Scrabble, frames of buildings, little red sports cars and more than anything else—other men. I am constantly thinking that someone has your color eyes, your shape nose, a face just like yours, but never quite so handsome. I miss you madly but I never want to see you again. However, you are still my Daddy.

Love forever,

(b) To Susan

You are the most possessive female I have met in my life. Your gall is only surpassed in its enormousness by your big mouth. You never cease to put your nose into other people's business. Instead you should take care of your own business which is in a greater need than that of the others you worry about. The perplexities of your life should be ample enough to keep you out of mischief. And last, but definitely not least, you'll get along with me better.

(c) Dear Mother,

As you know there has been a change in my character in the last few months. You probably noticed that I'm harder to get along with. I've been very edgy lately and sleep alot. I'm dropping out of school because its no longer important to me. All in all, I guess I just said the hell with society as a whole. My feelings are this because I am now a drug addict. Yes Mother, I am hooked on Dope. Right now and forever more, my only want, need, and desire will be for heroin. I'm really strung out and would rather die than rehabilitate.

It all started out in the very way almost every other junkie starts out. I was young and wild. I was ready to experience any new thing that seemed interesting. I sped through the first stage of alcoholism. I quickly moved to smoking reefers in the parks with the fellows. I enjoyed reefer smoking very much. It surprised me that you never found out about it. Then I took my first part of my last step. In the concrete jungle called New York I somewhat graduated. I moved up to heroin. I took my first blow (sniff) at about sixteen. I was always curious about the use of heroin. The addicts always did look look beautiful to me when they were in a deep nod. When I first used heroin the high was the best I ever had. (I went on to get better highs as I used more heroin but for the first time using it it was better than anything else I ever used.) As first I said to myself I shouldn't use this anymore. Mother it wasn't the fear of heroin itself, it was because I knew that after only trying it once I knew that I loved the high. However, I didn't stop so now I am one of the lowest species of man since God's creation.

I know that you won't understand Mother. It's very bad. The reason that I left home is because I didn't want to bring any disgrace on you or Pop. Also, I know that I am now a low person but I didn't want to sink as low as to steal from you, the person I love most in the world. Don't try to understand me Ma, its impossible. Right now at this very moment I am sick. I need to get me a shot of heroin. If I am lucky Mother, if I am very lucky, if God is looking down upon me now he knows what I mean by if I am lucky. Mother, if I am lucky I will take this shot and die of an overdose because I'm dead already and I don't bring nothing but hurt and pain to other people. And you didn't raise me to be like that.

Your son,

Just Writing 5

Look around you. Do you have vocabulary for whatever you can see? One word? A few words? Many words? Make a complete list of the words that have come into your mind during this exercise.

Does noticing yourself and what you are doing provide more words? Add them to your list.

Are you sure you have exhausted your vocabulary for what you can see and what you are doing? Is your list as complete as it could be?

* * *

Will any arrangement of two or more words on your list yield a sentence? Every possible arrangement of two or more words? Some arrangements but not others?

Do you consider some of your sentences "better" than others? Why?

How many different sentences can you make using only these words? (Each word may be used more than once.)

* * *

Make five separate and distinct sentences about whatever you can see using any words you wish.

Can these five sentences be arranged in order to make a complete statement?

Is any one particular order "better" than the others? Why?

* * *

Can the statement you made in the last exercise be expressed through a different choice of words? Can it be expanded into a much fuller statement? How? Can it be contracted into a much shorter statement? How?

Just Writing 6

Write rapidly for 10 minutes without stopping or pausing to make corrections. When you have finished writing, put the paper aside, without reading what you wrote, for at least 20 minutes.

Read what you wrote aloud, making sure that you do two things:

(1) Read exactly what is written on the paper.

(2) Listen to yourself reading and catch the points when what you hear fails to make sense or sounds "funny."

If you find anything that doesn't make sense, change the words so that it does make sense.

If you find anything that sounds funny, change it so that it sounds right.

When you finish, read the corrected copy over again to see if you need to make further changes.

Show your completed manuscript to someone else and ask them what they think.

* * *

Ask someone to read a few sentences to you from a book so that you can write them down. Each sentence should be dictated with normal speed and expression, and the person should not stop except at the end of each sentence.

After you have finished writing, ask the person to read the same sentences over again while you follow on your paper. See if all the little words have been included in what you wrote. Have any letters or syllables been left off the ends of words?

Give your paper to the other person and read from the book yourself while your helper checks what you wrote. See if your helper can catch anything you missed.

Have you noticed whether writing and proofreading require the same state of mind? Different states of mind?

Section II: Becoming a Writer

Samples of spontaneous composing followed by reading aloud, listening to oneself, and looking. All of the writers were students in "Developmental English" at The College of Staten Island. The corrections are written above the line.

(a) things were working for us I would go out, work for long period of time, [*not* above "were"] and when would come home your mother would always argue with [*I* above "would"] me, for not ~~been~~ home; but ~~you~~ would always try to give ~~her~~ and ~~you~~ [*being* above "been"; *I* above "you"; *you* above "her"; *her* above "you"] everything you ~~and her~~ need it. I try to be a good father but your mother [*all* above "and her"] was just too unfair to me I just couldn't take and I found it much easier [*it* above "take"] to leave the house for good, than just trying to live with someone I didn't lo~~ne~~ ~~anymore~~. [*v any more* above "lone anymore"]

(b) On monday when I went to work my friend peter came to me and told [*up* above "came"] that he told carmen that I like her. I told peter why did you had tell her [*me* above "told"; *d* above "like"; *to go and* above "had"] that, he reply because I want you to get together with her. But Peter I'm very happy that you want me to get together but you should have ask me [*with her* above "together"; *ed* above "ask"] first. But anyway what did she ~~said~~ when you told her that I like her. She [*say* above "said"] was excited and ~~told me to get your your~~ telephone number for ~~she~~ can [*asked me to get your* above crossed out text; *her so she* above "she"] call you. But why did you ask me for my telephone for and you waited [*number* above "telephone"] until her sister came up and ask me for it. And he told me I'm sorry Elvis [*ed* above "ask"] because I ~~forget~~. [*forgot* above "forget"]

(c) I am writing this letter to you about if I ~~had has~~ *have* paid the price that you mention*ed* at the beginning of the semester. In one way I've been playing the price but at the sametime I have been sick alot*,* ~~S~~*s*o I couldn't *have* been paying that much of the price*.* Like in attendance I haven't come to class much so that I ~~may~~ *can't* say that I paid the *full* price but when I have attend*ed* class most of the time I am wide awake and listening to what you ~~may been~~ *all* saying or ~~some of the people's~~ *someoneelse* in class. And sometimes I a*'m* not listening and it is like *if* my mind is somewhere else. But when it comes to participation in class I do participate*, like* when you ask me a question or if I have to read what I ~~writing~~ *wrote* out. Now if I work outside of class ~~yes~~ *? Y*es I have work*ed* outside of class*'* like whe~~re~~*n* you give an assignment to ~~it~~ *do. It* might be late when I give it to you but I am ~~working~~ *doing my work* outside of class. Sometime*s* I just forget to bring the work with *me* but I do your assignment anyway. Now from what I have ~~gotten~~ *learned* from this course is that I tend to write a little more than before. And I now look over *my work* sometime to recheck it so that I ~~know~~ *might know* where I have forgotten to write *a word or mispelled a word* And I thank you for what I have learn*ed* during this semester.

Section II: Becoming a Writer

The following is a sample of self-correction prompted by symbols in the margin which directed her attention to the places where she needed to look and listen more carefully.

       T   d M   S
~~t~~here was once this little girl name ~~m~~argaret ~~s~~he had a lot of pain and

                                         it   She
didn't know how to deal with ~~them~~. ~~her~~ didn't know how to make

           I
friends. ~~it~~ came so hard for her because people didn't like the way she

                                          W
talked. Because she came from down south. ~~w~~hen she tried to talk to

people they would make fun of her. So one day she told them that she

                                    had   make fun of
wanted to be their friend and if they ~~didn't had~~ to ~~laugh at~~ her then it

                                                         first
was no use. Because they was acting as if they were in the ~~1~~ grade. So

             then   good
they understood her and they became friends.

Just Writing

Practice Exercises for Rapid Growth in Writing

Writing in script was first introduced, if I remember rightly, in the third grade, and from then on written composition remained a major part of the school curriculum. In spite of almost daily practice, however, most of us were hardly more adept at fifteen than we had been at eight. Although some were better than others, of course, even the "best" students were still lacking in facility and apt to mutter and groan whenever writing was called for. Clearly, very little growth occurred during these years in spite of our teachers' earnest efforts to make it happen.

So it's obvious that most of what passed for "practice" simply wasn't capable of promoting growth. I don't really know if many other students ever experienced a growth spurt in writing. For my own part, I only began to make rapid progress in facility (and, to a lesser extent, in correctness) after I started writing poems and personal letters—forms of expression that were never part of the curriculum or ever graded or corrected.

So it must have been the case that I stumbled on something in these wholly extracurricular and spontaneous forms of writing that made them capable of promoting my growth.

When I compare "practice" in school with what I did on my own, I see a clear difference—and it isn't a matter of "motivation," for I wasn't a tuned out or turned off student. It's quite simply that when I was writing on my own, I set myself challenges that were compatible with the limited tools at my disposal. That is, I wrote only when I had something to say and in the choice of language that came easily to hand. As a result, I became increasingly able to get something down on paper that was about as lucid as my spoken speech. I always remained more inventive and facile as a talker, but the gap between speaking and writing narrowed.

"Practice," as it was interpreted in school, was something else. Teachers were always trying to plant something new in my head, whether it was rules of grammar, principles of organization, or bright ideas for making my writing more "concrete." The effect of such lessons was to distract me from drawing on my own resources since the lessons always reminded me of all the things I *didn't* know, and supposedly *should* know, in order to write.

It strikes me now that most people seldom, if ever, encounter the kind of practice exercises that mobilize what they have and promote rapid growth. So even if they begin well—either in the early grades or in a "remedial" class that dissolves their blocks against writing—they never get the practice they need to develop facility as writers. On the contrary, they are always being plunged into something new and distracting (linguistics, rhetoric, logic, literary models, etc.)

instead of being given the chance to exploit what they already have. As a result, they never find writing getting more manageable, only more complicated and mysterious. They write as laboriously at thirty-five as they did at fifteen.

So what is needed are practice exercises that enable a person to write with more ease and facility *immediately* with a small expenditure of time and without learning anything new.

It seems to me that any writing activity or exercise that satisfies the following criteria can function as a genuine practice exercise:

- It leaves the writer in no doubt, from the very beginning, that he or she has something appropriate to say;

- It provides the opportunity to find more to say as the writer goes along;

- It utilizes the writer's current resources as a speaker of his or her native language (whether "standard" or a "dialect") without trying to expand them;

- It imposes restrictions that free the writer from the responsibility to take care of everything at once;

- It forces the writer to focus on what he or she can do more or less spontaneously and prevents the writer from becoming inhibited by concern for what is unknown;

- It provides an opportunity for the writer to be more ambitious than last time.

When these criteria are truly respected, the basis for achieving rapid growth in writing is provided—the basis, that is, for growth in facility to the point that a person is able to write whatever he or she could utter in spoken speech.

Once a person has crossed this threshold many of the traditional preoccupations of linguistic and literary study become meaningful and helpful. But not before.

So part of becoming a writer is giving the necessary amount to time to practice of the kind that builds facility.

The following pages contain only a few examples of the kind of practice exercises that are necessary and sufficient for rapid growth toward the crucial first threshold. Readers are invited to invent as many more as common sense and creativity may dictate.

Exercises for Rapid Growth 1

Whenever you set aside any time for writing (especially if you are sitting down to do an assignment, compose a business letter, etc.) begin with this preliminary exercise:

(a) Start writing as soon as a first word[1], or phrase, or sentence, comes into your mind and continue moving your pencil (without pausing to "think" or "correct") as long as you have anything, however trivial, to say.

(b) After you have completed the above exercise four or five times, begin to keep a tally of the number of minutes you are able to sustain nonstop writing and the number of words produced.

(c) After you have completed the above ten times, begin to reread your entries (several days after they are written) and keep a tally of how many mistakes you detect.

Do you find that keeping track of what happens when you write has an influence on the result?

Are you finding that, as time goes on, your first burst or writing goes on longer?

Are you finding that this procedure helps you to become "warmed up" before you actually begin working on the task you are required to do?

Does the "warm up" take place even if what you write about in the nonstop composing is completely unrelated to the task required?

Do you find that you get more "warmed up" if you write about something that is not related to the assigned task? Or is the result better if you find yourself "brainstorming" in relation to the assignment?

---

1 Start writing immediately, whether or not the first thing that comes has anything to do with the task you are supposed to be working on.

Exercises for Rapid Growth 2

Wherever you are when you read this, force yourself to cover an entire page with writing NOW. If you can't think of anything to say, just write down all the isolated words you can think of. (If you can't think of any words, look around you and write down labels for whatever you can see.)

Repeat the above exercise as often as possible, in the greatest possible variety of circumstances and surroundings.

After you have completed the above exercise five or six times, keep a record of the amount of time it takes you to cover the page on each successive occasion.

* * *

If and when you reach the point where you can generate a sizeable number of words in a few minutes, write for ten minutes each day in a short notebook.[1] Try not to make corrections or revisions as you write or to reread your entries until they are at least a week old.

When you have filled the book, write your name and "Volume I" on the front cover and begin your second book …

Is this the first complete book you have ever written?

How do you feel now that you have completed an entire volume?

Is there anything in "Volume I" you would like to write more about? To rewrite in a more developed or correct form?

Does knowing that you now have a lot of material collected make you feel any different about writing?

---

1 The "blue books" used for examinations in schools and colleges (which contain about 16 pages) are ideal for this purpose. But any book of 50 pages or less will do. You might want to make your own by stapling a number of sheets together or folding a large sheet of wrapping paper.

Exercises for Rapid Growth 3

When you have writing you *must* do (essays for school, official correspondence, letter of application, etc.) begin working on the assigned task only after a "warm up" consisting of any *two* of the following exercises in quick succession.

- (a) A letter to a friend
- (b) A page of gripes or complaints
- (c) A poem
- (d) A list of words you seldom use because of uncertainty about the spelling (using the dictionary is permissible).

* * *

When you begin writing whatever you must for school or business, cover a page with random jottings on the subject, assignment, or task before attempting anything more formal or organized. The back of an envelope is good for this purpose.

Throw this away before continuing further.

> Do you find that you are made richer or poorer by throwing away your first writing? Is it easier or harder to continue with the assigned task after throwing away something you have already composed?

Repeat this exercise several times to see if your response to the questions is always the same.

Section II: Becoming a Writer

Exercises for Rapid Growth 4

Turn the following into a comic strip by adding to the drawings provided, supplying further pictures, and composing appropriate dialogue.

Continue the story in writing or start over and compose a short story based on the work you have already done above.

* * *

Write a story that builds up to this final line: "As I looked back, all I could see was the car and the grapefruit lying next to it on the road."

Exercises for Rapid Growth 5

Fill in the blank areas below.

The

My journal for this day _____, 20____

_____
_____
_____
_____
_____

> The people in *Another World* try *To Survive a Marriage* with *The Doctors in Somerset*. Their children are *The Young and the Restless*. They are *Search for Tomorrow*, looking for *All My Children*. In *Every Day of Our Lives* people drive to *Peyton Place*. At *General Hospital* they have *Only One Life to Live* and *The World Slowly Turns*.
>
> Staten Island Community College Student

Section II: Becoming a Writer

Exercises for Rapid Growth 6

Fill in each of the blanks below with one word or more.[1] When you finish, check to be sure that the paragraph makes sense and sounds like English.

The subject I want to discuss, _____, is seldom examined carefully, _____ it is not unimportant. _____ should not be neglected _____ we are not able to _____ and, I should add, _____. If given serious attention _____ likely to hold our _____ some time to come. _____ great minds in the _____ they were seldom satisfied _____ and we may fear _____ still I am certain _____ if we are brave _____ finally find the answer.

* * *

Fill in the blanks and finish the essay.

Frequently _____ that _____ however _____ that _____ even _____ to _____. When _____ and _____ that _____ the _____ which _____
_____
_____
_____
_____
_____
_____

---

[1] Some readers may find the passage provided too difficult. A similar challenge can be provided by selecting a paragraph that is within the reader's competence and crossing out every fifth word.

Exercises for Rapid Growth 7

Write a sentence (or paragraph) to each of the following specifications:

(1) To make others laugh

(2) To make them feel like crying

(3) To make them wonder

(4) To make them regret

(5) To make them admire your intelligence

(6) To make them respond to your soulfulness

(7) To make them sympathize with your weakness

(8) To make them recognize your uniqueness

(9) To let them know what you think of them

Transforming What One Writes

One thing I have learned by reading books about writing intended for college students is that most authors are most interested in one particular topic: setting out formal requirements for an acceptable piece of writing. Of course, hardly any two authors agree on the proper route to this great end. One presents a list of 200 errors and spends 200 pages describing all the mistakes you-must-not make. Another says that each theme must have a beginning, middle and end and spends 12 chapters telling you where the beginning begins, and how to recognize the middle of the middle, and anticipate the end of the end. Still another says you must delight your reader with visual images and impress her/him with five-syllable words. This author provides you with 400 pages of examples of the sort of thing he has in mind, all written by experienced people she thinks your teacher admires. However much the authors of composition texts disagree among themselves about what is THE approach, they all agree that the name of the game is "giving the man what he wants." And the reader learns that he too can become a qualified writer if he, or she, will just inscribe the proper formulas in his heart and on the walls of his study.

One trouble with all these wonderful bits of advice is that they tend to cancel each other out. One year an instructor raps you over the knuckles if you use "I," and the next year your teacher wants to hear about "My most intimate personal embarrassment." So you keep writing new formulas up on your wall and crossing them out again. And every year you have to knock your papers into shape with a totally new model in mind. Very confusing.

One day I set myself a small problem. I looked at a page of scattered thoughts I had jotted down a few weeks before, on a day when I was thinking about my experiences as a rider on the New York subways, and I asked myself a few questions: Could this be changed into an essay on the pace of contemporary life? Could this be developed into a short story? Could this become an example of reportage? Could I rewrite this so that "I" is never used? Could I recast this with a beginning, middle, and end and the requisite number of topic sentences? The answer to all of these questions seemed to be YES. Then I asked myself another question: Are there any considerations I need to be aware of no matter what sort of transformation I choose to make? Again, the answer seemed to be yes. So I set about trying to discover for myself the fundamental components of editing in all cases and under all circumstances. What I discovered is presented on the following pages.

Transforming Writing 1

Look out of the window and write one sentence about what you see.

Is it possible to change your sentence by adding more words at the end? At the beginning? If so, do it.

Is it possible to change your sentence by inserting additional words (or phrases) somewhere? Between every two words? If so, do it.

Can it be changed by omitting some of the original words?

Can it be changed further by retaining the original (or changed) words but rearranging their order?

Is it possible to restate the content of the original statement in another sentence, using a different selection of words?

✱ ✱ ✱

Take a paragraph you have already composed and change it through the addition, substitution, omission, and reordering of sentences. (You can do this either on paper, on a computer or tablet screen, or in your head).

✱ ✱ ✱

Take a page you have already composed and change it through the addition, substitution, omission, reordering, and restatement of paragraphs, in as many different ways as possible.

✱ ✱ ✱

Take a piece of writing (of several pages in length) that you have already composed and change it through the addition, substitution, reordering, and restatement of words, sentences, and paragraphs, in as many ways as possible. Make the changes in your head first. Then write the revised composition on the screen, or on paper, including only those changes you like.

Transforming Writing 2

Select a single sentence from something you have already written and determine how many different changes are possible on the basis of addition, insertion, omission, substitution, and reordering of words.

> Can all possible changes be considered as "improvements"?
>
> On what basis will you consider a particular change to be an improvement? Is this a question you have difficulty answering?

* * *

Select several paragraphs from something you have already written and consider transforming them in the light of the following questions:

> Is it possible to eliminate any words without altering the basic meaning? If so, does this sort of change result in an improvement? Is your answer true for all cases? Why?
>
> Is it possible to modify (that is, change slightly) the meaning by inserting or adding words to some of the sentences? If so, can doing this result in an improvement? When?
>
> Is it possible to insert or add more sentences that extend or expand the meaning? If so, can doing this result in an improvement? When?

* * *

Examine several pieces of writing you have already composed but not improved.

> Do you find any places where improvements seem to be particularly needed?
>
> Could you say that the improvements are generally required in some particular part? At the beginning? The middle? The end?
>
> Is there any particular part of your paragraphs that seems to require special attention and improvements? At the beginning? Elsewhere?

Transforming Writing 3

Construct a "still life" out of common household objects such as dishes, utensils, etc. and place it on a table top.

Compose a one-sentence description of what you see.

> Is what you have written *true*? How do you know?
>
> Test the *adequacy* of what you have written by reading what you have written about to someone who has not seen your still life, and ask them to construct an identical display on the basis of your description.
>
> If your original statement was demonstrably inadequate, see if you can make whatever changes are necessary to make it adequate before testing again.
>
> Have you observed the sorts of changes that lead to greater adequacy? What are they?
>
> Is what you have written both adequate and *economic*? Could the same content be expressed with fewer words? Experiment to find out.
>
> Is what you have written *correct* and *right*? That is, does it sound like the English you hear and speak? Test to see if what sounds "right" to you also sounds "correct" to someone else.
>
> Is it possible for you to make what you have written "beautiful," "vivid," or "intriguing"? What sorts of changes seem necessary to achieve these results?

Can the following three words be transformed into a moving statement, an absurd statement, a delightful statement, or a witty statement?

> She died yesterday.

> Was making these changes only a matter of finding words and juggling them?
>
> Did you need to alter your own mood in order to make each transformation? In order to think about making it?
>
> Was mental imagery required in order to make the changes?
>
> Would you conclude, on the basis of this page, that transforming requires additional components besides those mentioned in exercises 1 and 2?

* * *

Transforming Writing 4

When you are composing a first draft, is it a requirement that whatever you say must make sense? Is it the same when you rewrite or edit?

* * *

When you are composing, is it a requirement that all of what you say belongs in the order in which it first comes to mind? Is it the same when you rewrite and edit?

* * *

When you are composing, it is a requirement that whatever you say be adequate to express what you have in mind? Is it the same when you rewrite and edit?

* * *

When you are composing, is it a requirement that you deliberately select the vocabulary that most precisely and economically expresses what you have in mind? Is it the same when you rewrite and edit?

* * *

When you are composing, is it a requirement that whatever you say sounds correct and right? Is it the same when you rewrite and edit?

* * *

When you are composing is it a requirement that whatever you write be your final word on the subject? Is it the same when you rewrite or edit? Always?

* * *

When you are composing, is it a requirement that you take others—your potential readers—into account? Is it the same when you rewrite and edit? Always?

* * *

Is spelling equally important in composing and editing? Punctuation? Neatness and legibility?

Transforming Writing 5

Observe yourself during the following exercises to see how your internal mental climate is altered or affected by the demands of each successive phase.

(a) Write continuously for three minutes on the first topic that comes to mind, without stopping to make changes or corrections.

(b) Transform the results into a paragraph in which all of the sentences are complete and belong together in the order you have chosen.

(c) Write again for three minutes on any topic you wish without making changes or corrections.

(d) Transform your "free writing" as you did the first time.

(e) Merge the two paragraphs into a single, meaningful unit. You may need to make many changes to achieve this result.

Did you catch yourself preparing inwardly to function in a different way each time you shifted from "composing" to "transforming" and back again?

Can you say, "I know, from inside, the state I need to be in in order to write or rewrite"?

Did you ever need to remind yourself of what you were doing in order to keep in the appropriate state?

When did you feel more in contact with the movement of your thoughts—during composing or editing?

When did you feel more sensitive to language—during composing or editing?

Can you conclude, on the basis of this exercise, whether you relate more easily to composing or editing?

* * *

Observe yourself as an editor over a period of time in the light of the following questions:

Do you know yourself as someone who can be intoxicated by his/her own words? So much so that you need to "sober up" before you can edit them?

Do you know yourself as someone who becomes so attached to your own expression that to discard or change causes pain?

Do you know that the words you have already written may be endowed with the power to suggest a new and different meaning to you when you return to them after an absence?

Do you know yourself as capable of destroying what you have composed through the process of zealous editing?

Transforming Writing 6

Additional exercises for practice in transforming writing:

Compose a dramatic dialogue between two angry people. Cross out all the statements made by one of the speakers. Construct a monologue in which the remaining speaker does all the talking and anticipates (and answers) the missing speaker's objections.

* * *

Choose an article from a newspaper or magazine. Copy each sentence of the article on a separate slip of paper.

Shuffle the slips.

Assemble a new article by placing the slips in a sequence that makes sense.

Compare the new arrangement with the original to see which you prefer and why.

This could also be done using Copy and Paste on a computer.

* * *

Select a sample of your own writing—something you believe is finished.

Examine (and, when necessary, change) each and every word, sentence and paragraph until you are perfectly satisfied that you are capable of making no further improvements.

Count how many changes you have made.

Repeat the exercise often and compare results.

* * *

Write a paragraph of at least 250 words.

Reduce the length by cutting out as many words as possible without destroying the basic meaning.

Replace the remaining words by one sentence that contains the essence of your original paragraph.

Replace your sentence by one word that sums up all that you wished to say.

Using the word as a title, compose a sentence that introduces the thought(s) implicit in it.

Expand the sentence into a new paragraph.

Section II: Becoming a Writer

Mastering the Mechanics of Writing

When I was a kid in school the "mechanics" of writing were my weakness. Although my mistakes weren't so numerous (nor so consistent) as those of many of the students I teach now, I was definitely a "bad" writer in the technical sense. In fact, my teachers used to say the same things about me that I hear colleagues muttering about their students today—that I needed to learn about complete sentences, agreement in number and tense, spelling, punctuation, etc. Well, they did their best to set me straight on all those points, but I never benefited much. I just kept on making the same mistakes year after year.

If I try to assign a date to the period when I first began to display some improvement in mechanics, I find that it more or less coincides with the time when I learned touch typing, started working as my father's secretary (taking dictation and transcribing his manuscripts), and worked on the high school literary magazine as an editor and proofreader.

It's tempting to think that my writing improved because I had renewed "motivation" to master the mechanics, but this explanation really won't do since I had already been interested and motivated for years previously without visible effect. As a matter of fact, I was viewed by my teachers as something of a mystery; they just couldn't figure out how the only boy in the school who was serious about writing and literature could be one of the worst writers!

What practical experience in secretarial and editorial work did for me—I see now with the aid of hindsight—was to clarify the functional difference between two components of the writing process that had remained seemingly indistinguishable previously: *composition* and *transcription*. Until I became a typist taking down someone else's words, I never realized that "writing" could be seen as a joint and collaborative effort between my voice, which composes, and my hand, which transcribes. Nor had I perceived that each of these had its own "mechanics." First there is the seemingly spontaneous mechanism of voice production by which images, thoughts, etc. are transformed into complex trains of sound in which intonation, phrasing, melody, and rhythm are as important as the words they carry. Second there is the less spontaneous transformation by which a single component of the voice—words—is extracted from the flow of sound and transferred, via the hand and fingers, into a visual coding.

I think it's true to say that prior to this time I thought of writing only in terms of composing, of inventing what I wanted to say through the mechanics of my voice. That what I had in my throat to say couldn't be transferred to the page without special concern for the mechanics of manual transcription simply hadn't occurred to me. Although I had been "writing" for years, I had never grasped the simple fact that having something to say at the tip of my tongue is not the same thing as setting it down on paper, or up on a screen, faithfully. Transcribing words accurately requires mastery of a mechanics that has nothing to do with literary creation or expression *per se*, only with its transfer into a written code. In essence, this is a matter of finding practical techniques for using one's fingers, sight, and hearing to mediate between an activity that is swift and spontaneous (composing) and an activity that is slow and laborious (transcribing).

In becoming a typist I acquired certain mechanical functionings that, had I learned them earlier, would surely have made a great impact on my writing skills:

> I learned how to use my hearing as a precise instrument for receiving what was said so that I could hold an exact memory of the train of words that needed to be transcribed.

> I learned how to use my fingers as an efficient system for setting words down on paper.

> I learned how to use my vocal, hearing, and visual powers as a single, integrated system for proofreading whatever I committed to paper.

Soon, I was employing these same functionings in relation to my own composing as well—both when I was typing and writing in longhand.

Although I succeeded in mastering the mechanics of transcription in the way I have described, I can't claim that I made use of my own experience when I became a teacher. For although I was always skeptical about the utility of instruction in grammar and usage, many years passed before I recognized that there was an alternative approach to the mechanics of writing that had worked for me and might have an application to others.

The penny dropped, so to speak, only when I suddenly noticed that something that was true for me was also true for all of my students with "problems" in grammar and usage. *Their speech was invariably more consistent and sensitive than their writing.* However many mistakes people might make in speaking, there were always many more when they came to write. And when students progressed to a point where they wrote as well as they spoke, the product, while far from perfect in many cases, was *always* a distinct improvement in comparison with previous writing.

This observation, so obvious in retrospect, led me to the conclusion that it is the mechanics of transcription—the proper use of hearing, sight, and hands—which students of writing have most trouble with, not the mechanics of speech. This is why their writing invariably contains a far greater quantity of errors than their talking. Their writing is "bad" grammatically for the same reason that mine was— because what they do in the process of getting words down on paper is inadequate as a vehicle for whatever they compose with their voice. And the most efficient way for them to improve the grammar and usage that shows up in their writing is to work on what they do when they transcribe rather than to seek linguistic instruction.

Section II: Becoming a Writer

The pages that follow this introduction contain practical exercises I have found useful in coping with the basic challenge of transcription—that the hand is so much slower and more clumsy that the voice. Each page has a specific focus and bears upon one or more of the functionings required by the mechanics of transcription.

> I must be able to use my fingers efficiently, and with an economy of effort, so that the interval between voicing and transcribing words is as brief as possible.
>
> I must be able to hear precisely what I say so that words, and parts of words (especially endings) can be held correctly in mind until the hand is able to transcribe them with nothing left out.
>
> I must be able to hear and interpret the nonverbal vocal elements of speech (especially phrasing and intonation) so that I can sense the need for punctuation and supply it.
>
> I must be able to hold sizable trains of words long enough for my hand to catch up to my voice.
>
> I must be able to consult my mental and somatic images of words so that I can both spell them correctly and detect misspellings.
>
> I must be able to use my voice, hearing, and sight as a single functioning system for identifying the mistakes that are inevitable given the nature of transcription.

When all of these functioning are present, and only then, can a writer hope to master the mechanics of transcription and be able to write as correctly as he or she speaks.

Two words of caution are also necessary:

(1) "Good" grammar, spelling, and punctuation, however dear to the hearts of teachers, editors, parents, and critics of the educational establishment, are far less important than composing. Transcription only matters because one already has something to say and wants to get it down faithfully. Since most of us have to be our own secretaries most of the time, some mastery of the mechanics is indispensable. But concern with faithful transcription easily becomes exclusive and inhibits the writer (especially the beginning writer) altogether—a situation so common that it is the rule rather than the exception in most people's experience of studying writing. For this reason, it is essential to remember that most professional authors continue, throughout their careers, to be better at composing than at transcribing. They never cease requiring some secretarial assistance in order to be "correct." Since this is true of them, shouldn't it be kept in mind by *every* writer?

(2) Given the nature of English grammar and spelling, perfection in the mechanics of transcription is seldom possible for any writer and is a frustrating goal to pursue. It is more intelligent to seek not perfection but improvement—to be content when one is able to make fewer mistakes during the process of transcription and to proofread more carefully. Since most writers, especially beginning students of writing, make a great many mistakes in transcription, even a small improvement is equivalent to mastery.

Mechanics 1

Focus on the muscle tone in your arms, hands, fingers, and abdomen as you start to write in order to know, from inside, what somatic state accompanies this activity.

> Would you describe the state in which you usually begin writing as "loose" or "tight"?
>
> Have you found your habitual state conducive to writing?
>
> At the moment when you begin, do you feel that you are performing an act of "surrender" or "attack"? Does it make any difference?
>
> Does your state change as you continue writing?

* * *

Wherever you are when you read this, take a writing implement and begin "writing" immediately by making continuous scribbles or swirls on a sheet of paper. Continue for several minutes before reading the questions below.

> Are you in the same state as when you write normally?
>
> Does this exercise tell you something about the amount of physical energy generally wasted when you write?

* * *

Practice starting to write by making scribbles on paper for a few minutes before you begin transcribing words.

> Does this exercise seem to lead to greater conservation of energy when you write?
>
> Would you consider changing any of your established habits in the light of your experience with the exercises on this page?

One Person's Experiment:

Mechanics 2

Choose a topic on which you can write easily and compose for a few minutes, experimenting at the same time with different ways of grasping your pencil.

Is your control over the pencil affected when you grasp it closer or farther away from the point? Can you locate the place from which it is possible to manipulate the instrument with the least effort?

Can the amount of tension or pressure with which you grip your pencil be varied? Is it possible to loosen your grip without a corresponding loss of control? Will such adjustments affect the amount of energy needed for writing?

Do adjustments in the location and firmness of your grip affect the speed or legibility of your handwriting?

Is it possible to adjust the angle formed by your writing instrument and the surface of the paper? Is any particular adjustment to be preferred from the point of view of reducing friction between paper and pencil?

Are any of your established habits of holding a pen or pencil shaken by this experiment?

Do you now know how you may use your hand in order to maximize output and minimize fatigue?

* * *

Compose continuously for five minutes, alternating between print and script in one-minute segments.

Which requires a greater number of muscular movements—printing or script? How many more?

Which way results in great productivity as measured by the number of words transcribed in a set period of time?

Which demands that you be more conscious of your physical movements? Of the appearance of words on the page?

Which allows you to remain in more continuous contact with the sense or meaning of whatever you wish to transcribe?

Do you now have a basis for deciding when to use script or printing?

Section II: Becoming a Writer

> If you try writing with the wrong hand, the one unaccustomed to writing, you may be better able to feel which muscles are used in writing.

> PRINTING TAKES A LOT MORE ENERGY THAN IF YOU WERE DOING IT IN SCRIPT

Mechanics 3

Give dictation to someone else in order to find answers to the following questions:

> If you compose in speech slowly enough for your secretary to take down each word as it is said, is it possible for you to keep pace with your thoughts as they come?
>
> If you compose slowly enough for your secretary to take down what you said word-by-word, are you able to be sure that your sentences "sound like English" without going over them several times?
>
> If you work so slowly, will you have the time and patience required to continue dictating until several pages are filled?
>
> Do your answers to these questions tell you why many slow and careful writers have trouble making sense and commit many errors in spite of the care they take?

* * *

Take dictation from someone else in order to find answers to the following questions:

> Can you possibly transcribe the words of a sentence accurately if you start writing the moment the person dictating to you begins speaking (at normal speed) and write as fast as you can to keep up?
>
> Will you have more success if you listen to all of the words of a single sentence, and take in its meaning as a whole, before you begin transcribing?

* * *

Experiment with taking dictation from yourself[1] in order to find answers to the following questions?

> Is it helpful to attempt to retain a mental image of whatever the sentence is about? Are you better able to hold the words in mind if you have an image of their content?
>
> After the words have been uttered, can you retain an "echo" of the melody and intonation of the sentence inside you? If so, does this help you to hold or recapture the words?
>
> If some of the original words have been lost, can speaking again the words you do retain trigger some of the rest?
>
> Do your answers to the questions above suggest any techniques you might practice as aids in transcription?

---

1 Say it first, a whole sentence at a time, then write it down.

Section II: Becoming a Writer

Mechanics 4

Practice uttering sentences to yourself and repeating them again (both aloud and in your head) without making any alterations.

> Do you find that you need to work on this in order to hold a sentence as long as this one accurately in mind?
>
> Does it help if you increase the amount of energy you put into expression and intonation and if you exaggerate the stress given to key words?
>
> Does it help if you emphasize the grouping of words in phrases instead of emphasizing each word alone?

* * *

Practice uttering sentences to yourself with stress on the sound that comes at the end of each word.

> Is this a part of words you need to be particularly conscious of in normal conversation or does it come automatically?
>
> Is this a part of words that is significant for writing? If so, why?
>
> Will you transcribe more accurately if you take care to listen particularly to the ends of words as you say them?

* * *

Practice listening to yourself uttering sentences in order to answer the following questions:

> Are the ends of all words equally important?
>
> Are there certain words whose endings are particularly important?
>
> Are there certain endings one finds attached to many words? Do they always have the same significance?
>
> Try to answer these questions by *listening and reflecting on what you hear* rather than recalling rules and explanations you have learned before.

Mechanics 5

Experiment to see whether the following techniques can help you to become a more accurate transcriber of your own sentences.

When you compose (in your head or out loud) put as much expression into your words as possible—try to move your whole body in rhythm with what you have to say.

When you compose a sentence, repeat it at least once to yourself before writing it down, focusing on the melody and intonation of each phrase —as if you were learning your lines in a play or teaching yourself a song.

When you start to transcribe a sentence, scribble the first phrase as quickly as possible as if you were writing a single word. Leave as little space as possible between each word and the next.

Transcribe in phrases, each of which must be taken down in one burst of activity without pausing or stopping for any reason.

As you transcribe each phrase, press more firmly on your writing implement whenever you come to a word your voice would cause to "stand out" if you were speaking the same phrase aloud.

> Do you find that working in this way helps you to retain more of the words?

> Do you ever find that a phrase triggers the one that comes after it? Or that a part triggers the rest?

If you look back over what you have transcribed, is there an "echo" of the original inside you, that helps you to locate and identify missing phrases, words, or parts of words?

* * *

Observe yourself when you are transcribing and notice whether any of your words or phrases are being expressed by your lips (silently or out loud) or by a movement of the pencil in the air, without a corresponding movement of your pencil on the page? If so, see if you can catch yourself at the exact moment when something "escapes" you in this way.

* * *

Practice saying longer and longer sentences to yourself and transcribing them phrase by phrase. Experiment to see if you are able to become so much concerned with phrases that you hardly notice the individual words at the moment when you are transcribing them.

Mechanics 6

Observe yourself transcribing and notice whether your flow is ever inhibited (or stopped) as you approach words that come easily into your mouth but that you are not sure you can spell. See if you can catch the muscles in your hand stiffening as you approach these words.

> Can you deliberately relax at the first sign of stiffening and continue transcribing, knowing that completing your sentence is more important that spelling each word correctly?

> Does the stiffening show that you have developed habits that prevent your writing from appearing as intelligent as your speech?

* * *

Write upside down (or backwards) in order to find answers to the following questions:

> Do you have an imagery in your mind that guides you in transcribing all the words you know the look of?

> Does it seem that the muscles in your fingers somehow "know" or possess a "feel for" the shapes of familiar words?

> Do these "imageries" function for words you don't know the look of, although you may be able to pronounce them correctly?

> Does it seem likely that you can spell words for which you lack a distinct "mental photograph"?

> Does it seem likely that you are able to pronounce many more words than you can spell correctly.... no matter how good a speller you are?

* * *

Practice making mental "photographs" of words. This is a matter of projecting an image of the word on an otherwise blank screen in your mind. (You will only confuse yourself if you try to recite the names of the letters at the same time—so don't try.)

After you are able to evoke a picture of how the word looks in your mind, "write" it out in the air with your finger—but without saying the names of the letters to yourself.

> Do you find that this technique can improve your spelling of common words you need to know?

Mechanics 7

Listen, from a distance of 20 feet or so, to someone who is speaking fluently, without hesitating in his or her choice of words. Try to focus on the train of sound you hear without necessarily hearing the exact words.

> Can you detect the beginnings and ends of sentences? Can you hear what the speaker's voice does to signal the beginning of a sentence? The end?

> Are the beginnings and ends of sentences signaled only by pauses and the absence of pauses? Or does the intonation of the voice play a part as well?

> Can you detect pauses and shifts in intonation within sentences that are apparently required by the meaning of what is said?

> Even without knowing precisely what the person is saying, could you sense with your ear where marks of punctuation would be needed if you were transcribing his or her utterance?

* * *

Practice listening to yourself, when you are speaking fluently and without hesitation, in order to catch how your own voice functions to indicate the beginnings and ends of sentences as well as significant pauses within sentences.

> Is it easier or more difficult to listen to your own voice?

> Will it help if you exaggerate expression, phrasing and intonation so that your voice resembles an actor performing a script rather than a normal speaking voice?

> Will it help if you not only listen to your own voice but also attempt to feel, from inside, what your voice is doing?

* * *

After you have written something down, read it over out loud with as much expression as possible. Exaggerate, as if you were an actor performing a script.

> Do you find that you are able to locate where each sentence should begin and end, even if you punctuated it incorrectly when you first wrote it down? Does your voice give you a "feel" for where periods, question marks, and exclamation marks should be?

> Do you find that you are able to locate the significant pauses within sentences that require some mark of punctuation?

> Do you find that working in this way leads to more frequent or less frequent marks of punctuation than previously? Have you been using more periods and commas than you need to or too few?

Mechanics 8

When you look at something which you have written, do you know that you can examine it, word-by-word, and both see and hear what is actually there? For example, are you alert to each of the word in this particular sentence or are you being carless?

Did you notice anything unusual about the sentence above? If not, look again.

* * *

Practice examining specimens of your own writing with such care that you note the sound and appearance of *every single word*. (It will probably help to place a check just above each word after you have examined it.)

* * *

Use your voice, hearing, and sight to comprehend the following sentences and see where improvement might be made:

To the too easily tried to try is too trying to the tried however no trying is

One won one and two won two

Can you be equally alert in examing spesimens of you're righting?

Testing Oneself as a Writer

Each time I go into the kitchen to prepare a meal I can't help but notice certain things about my ability as a cook: whether I am more deft with the utensils than I was yesterday; whether I work faster and more efficiently so that I require less energy to do the same or a greater amount of work than last time; whether I am more creative so that I can achieve better results with less costly materials and make sensible use of what is readily available instead of relying on exotic ingredients and elaborate equipment; whether I have renewed confidence in my own know-how to try unfamiliar dishes or impart new zest to the old standbys in my repertoire.

I don't say that I am conducting a "test" of my cooking ability on each of these occasions, but I am. Because cooking is something that matters to me, I take the opportunity to check how I'm doing at the same time that I'm doing it. And in testing myself I have at least two major criteria in mind. In the first place, I want to know if I am achieving a better performance today than yesterday. Have I, for example, produced a more delicious and tender stew than the last time? On a particular occasion I may find that the answer is, "No. I haven't. The meat was dry and tough even though I used a very good bottle of wine." But I don't necessarily conclude that my cooking ability is unimproved (or decreased) by this apparent disaster. I have, in fact, a second criterion that matters more to me than the first: have I become more aware of what I'm doing? Thus I may come to learn that my stew was barely edible because I used too much liquid and that I must be watchful of the amount of wine added during the cooking. A component of stew-making that was wholly hit-or-miss up to now has suddenly become a matter for conscious deliberation, experimentation, and practice. So I now know better what I'm doing when I set out to make a stew even though tonight's dinner seems, on the taste of it, to prove my incompetence.

Each time I become aware of a new component of what I'm doing, or reach the stage where a component that formerly required my constant watchfulness is dealt with seemingly "automatically," my ability as a cook is enhanced. Although my performance may remain clumsy and what I produce may still be far from satisfactory, my mental preparation for growth in cooking has advanced a step. And each time I am able to use my time in the kitchen to become more conscious of what cooking demands, and what I do with myself to meet these demands, I consider that I have taken another test and passed it.

Writing is just like cooking. I don't need to set aside special occasions for "testing" because I have a perfect opportunity to examine myself as a writer each time I work at my desk. Even if what I produce isn't a visible improvement on yesterdays' work—and it often is not—I am able to find out whether my mental preparation for writing has advanced by observing myself in the light of questions such as these:

Are components of the writing process that formerly required my constant watchfulness and conscious intervention at every moment more "automatic" today?

Am I aware, for the first time today, of additional components that require my watchfulness and conscious intervention?

Am I more able to utilize my mistakes as feedback indicating the areas where greater consciousness is needed instead of regarding them as accidents that "shouldn't have happened"?

Having said all the above, I have to admit that I often resist taking responsibility for testing myself. Although knowing that the only true test of where I am is my consciousness of what I do, I still want to be "tested" in the manner of the schools—that is, on the basis of performance alone. Instead of asking myself whether I know what I'm doing and whether I know better now than I knew earlier, I want to be given a formal "test," which someone else has made up. I want to be told, "Yes, you have satisfied the objectives laid down by the experts and are doing well."

Knowing that others are like me, reluctant to take responsibility for themselves and eager to satisfy the criteria set by others, I have formulated a "Self-test of Basic Writing" to conclude this section on "Becoming a Writer." I hope, however, that the test I have invented is a compromise between two levels of testing. My test is not only intended to enable writers to evaluate themselves on the basis of certain performance criteria but to probe their state of inner preparedness for all future writing.

Self-test of Basic Writing

I.

A. Can you look around at this moment and say what you see? Can you also write down what you said without changing it?[1]

B. Can you look inside yourself at this moment and say what you think and feel? Can you also write down what you have to say without changing it?

C. Can you make up lies and write them down?

D. Can you write down *anything* you are capable of speaking?

—If you can provide evidence to show that your answer to each of the questions above is "yes," you are a *writer*.

II.

A. Can you examine whatever you have already written to determine whether it makes sense?

B. Can you examine it and determine whether you have used enough words to express your meaning adequately?

C. Can you examine it and determine whether it sounds like spoken English?

D. Can you examine it and determine whether it sounds like your own voice when you speak in a certain way?

E. Can you make alterations in light of the questions above?

—If you can provide evidence to show that your answer to each of the questions above is "yes," you are an *editor*.

---

[1] The questions under I. should be answered without regard to spelling or punctuation.

Section II: Becoming a Writer

III.

A. Can you examine something you have written, edited, and recopied to determine whether any words or portions of words have been changed or omitted?

B. Can you determine that every mark of punctuation makes sense and is necessary to assist your readers in putting the proper voice into what you wrote?

C. Can you locate and correct the presence of careless errors if someone else indicates the line in which they appear? If the error is underlined (but not corrected)?

—If you can provide evidence to show that your answer to each of these questions is "yes," you are a *proofreader.*

IV.

How would you rate yourself as a *writer, editor,* and *proofreader*?

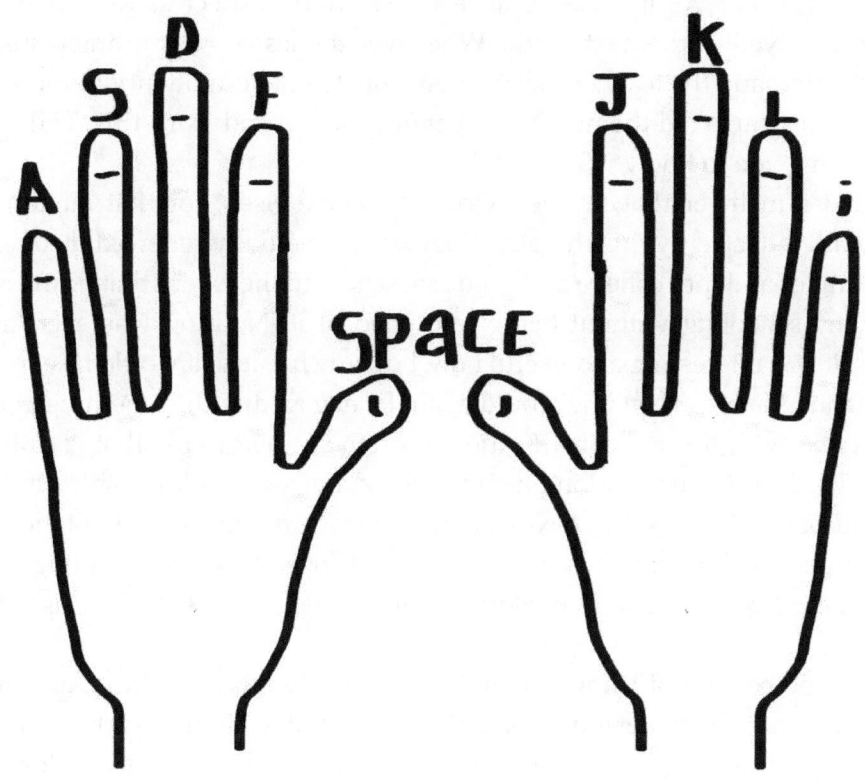

Section III:
Studies for the Enhancement of Writing

This section contains exercises and activities for people wishing to advance beyond the first threshold of writing, those for whom writing whatever they can say is not enough. Two of the chapters are rather long because the topics are rich and complex. In addition, there is a balance between purely practical and theoretical concerns—as is appropriate in a section for "advanced" students of writing and language.

Starting Points for Exploring the Universe of Writing

When I was in primary school, we were always being told that we had to do this or that—whatever it was—because THEY would expect us to have done it when we arrived in the next grade. Whenever the lesson was uninteresting or unproductive, and the teacher didn't know how to hold our attention, she would return to that same old theme: "You'd better wake up and learn this. THEY will be expecting you to know it."

I can't remember that my behavior (or anyone else's, for that matter) was particularly affected by this threat. Still, it was perpetually renewed throughout all the grades and into college and graduate school to the extent that I can't recall any of my schooling without being reminded of it. Nothing was ever taught because it was interesting and useful now, but only because it would be expected or demanded later—when one would again be engaged with something equally remote, and with the same justification. It often seemed to me that learning in school was like a journey along a straight and narrow track in which nothing mattered but arriving at the next station. My learning outside school, however, was completely different. It was like being set loose to wander in huge open fields where I could pause to explore whatever was immediately intriguing or challenging.

In my perception of things, such "academic" studies as writing, arithmetic, and calisthenics were set out along this road. But activities such as talking, figuring out how to spend a few cents wisely, or swimming were fields to be explored. The former were inherently uninteresting and needed to be justified by the argument that the journey onward could not proceed without them. The latter, however, needed no specific justification since I was doing them whenever I got a chance and finding more and more in them to do. Talking, for example, was a vast field—a universe, in fact—containing so much to challenge and delight in learning names for things, making up nonsense, impersonating adults, or constructing narratives based on my own experience. I know that my exploration of this universe was enhancing me and making me richer *now*. And this sense of expansion and enrichment enabled me to face the future confidently, ready to meet whatever might come or THEY might ask to me.

Although writing first entered my consciousness as a set of hurdles my teachers had placed here and there along the track, hurdles over which I often stumbled (as in the case of spelling and grammar), my sense of it changed in time. Several extraordinary teachers helped me to see that written expression was not only a "school subject" but also a rich field of experience that I was free to explore on my own. Further, they made me aware of the existence of "writers," people for whom this activity was not only a bountiful field but THE primary universe.

Section III: The Enhancement of Writing

I was shocked to discover that for some of them at least, writing was a concern so consuming and inclusive that they were willing to disregard everything else—friendship, economic security, respectability, etc. And in finding out that writing was a universe for them, I glimpsed the possibility that it might be so for me as well.

My own experience as a writer and a teacher has shown me that writing becomes truly interesting for everyone when it is perceived as a universe instead of a sequence of skills which THEY expect of us; when, in fact, it is approached in the same way we approach anything that holds the possibility of engaging us here and now. The exercises and activities on the following pages are, therefore, intended to open up the field of writing by providing practical opportunities to reflect upon such questions as the following:

> How does a person who explores this universe spend his or her time?
>
> Can I know myself and my powers better through writing?
>
> Can writing enhance my life in the present?
>
> How broad and how deep is this field?
>
> What does writing contribute to the human community?

It is not necessary to dedicate oneself exclusively to authorship in order to enter and explore the universe of writing. But anyone who has reached the threshold of being able to write whatever he or she can say is equipped to study what this field offers in the way of experience to the one with time to spend in it. Whether one chooses to explore only briefly or to dedicate one's life to knowing this universe, the opportunity is still open to find out something of what it is, to get a glimpse of what writers find in it, and to discover how their inner and outer lives are affected by it.

The Universe of Writing 1

Look at something you encounter every day (a piece of furniture, a view from a window, etc.) and transcribe on paper whatever images, associations, or thoughts come into your mind at *this* moment.

> Has your sight been enriched by the above activity—that is, have you seen more in these familiar surroundings as a consequence of preparing yourself to write about them?
>
> During the moments when you were summoning something to say, did you find that your ordinary perception of the things around you was enhanced? Were you "more observant," than usual? (You may need to repeat the experiment to be sure.)
>
> Once you started to write down your impressions, did you find that access to your inner store of images and ideas was greater than usual? Did you find that you continued to think of more things to say even though you were no longer relying on the environment to trigger images in your mind?
>
> Could you say, on the basis of this experience, that writing makes you more intensely aware of what is outside and inside you? A little more? Much more?

* * *

Observe someone passing on the street and make him or her the basis for a page of writing (or more than a page, if you wish).

> When you began writing, did you feel that you had enough "material" for a page?
>
> Did the act of writing draw more out of you than you at first supposed was there? Was every thought you have written down available when you began? Have any thoughts arrived and been lost while you were writing?
>
> Now that you are finished, do you feel that the process of filling a page has emptied you? Are you more or less energized than when you began?
>
> Could you say, on the basis of this experience, that writing makes you richer or poorer?

* * *

Observe yourself writing over a period of time before answering the following question:

> Do I ever feel physically expanded by the activity of writing?

The Universe of Writing 2

Before you go to sleep, try to recapture and recall on paper as many of the happenings of one day as you can.

> Has *this* day, which you have recorded, acquired more significance than other days?
>
> Does this day feel any richer than other days?

* * *

Reread what you wrote in the previous exercise after an interval of several days.

> How are you affected by looking back at what you wrote?
>
> Do you feel any link with that day? Do the days you *didn't* write about feel so close?

* * *

Keep a journal for several days in which you note down anything that strikes you as unusual, peculiar, or somehow memorable.

> Have you been more observant of life around you during the period during which you kept this journal?
>
> Have you been any more aware of your thoughts and feelings during this period?
>
> Has the keeping of the journal affected the intensity of your living during these few days?
>
> Does rereading what you have written, after an interval of a day or so, contribute anything to your experience? Does it affect your view of yourself?

The Universe of Writing 3

Write a letter to someone you feel strongly about.

> Is this an exercise you can do spontaneously? Or must you first create the mood in yourself that puts you in contact with the person to whom you are writing?

* * *

Write letters, in quick succession, to three different people.

> Are you exactly the same in each letter? Or must you make a new adjustment of your personality each time?

* * *

Write a letter, a fictional story, and an essay on the subject of "coincidence"

> Are you the same when you work on each of these?
>
> Does your mood change as you shift from one task to the next? Do you use the same selection of words each time? Do you speak in the same voice each time?

* * *

Could you say, on the basis of the activities on this page that writing makes you a more versatile person? More aware of your versatility?

The Universe of Writing 4

Choose one of the following forms of writing and prepare the best example of it that you can:

>a tale

>an essay

>a speech

>a proverb

>a review

>an argument

Have you chosen a familiar or unfamiliar form? Does your choice reveal something about you?

Have you chosen to express yourself directly or indirectly? Does this choice reveal something about you?

Have you exploited the full range of your vocabulary in your writing or only those words that came most readily to hand and that you were sure you could spell? Does this say something about you?

Have you made your piece as long and well-developed as possible? As short and succinct as possible? Does this say something about you?

Do you feel at peace with what you did? Is this also an expression of you?

* * *

Choose the form of writing above that seems *least* suited to your personality and gifts and see what you can make of it.

Do you feel you have made this form "yours"? Or is it still alien?

Have you taken any risks?

Has doing this exercise revealed anything to you about yourself?

* * *

Write something in which you deliberately adopt the voice of another person:

>a friend whose voice you know well

>a person who writes English with difficulty.

>a character on television or in a book you have read

>a well-known person whom you dislike

Is expressing the character and voice of someone else any less an expression of you as a writer?

Have you found that you can be as involved with someone else's voice as with your own?

Has your participation in this exercise revealed anything to you about yourself?

Section III: The Enhancement of Writing

The Universe of Writing 5

Fill out the following form as indicated:

Love is _____.

Love is _____.

Love is _____.

Love is _____.

Love is _____.

Were you initially mobilized or alienated by this exercise? Does your attitude reveal anything about your view of writing?

Did completing this exercise limit your creativity?

Did this exercise free you in any way?

* * *

Write an essay consisting of 22 sentences, each of which contains 22 words. The word "and" may only be used twice in any one sentence.

* * *

Write on any subject you choose and in any style you wish. You may also determine the length of your composition.

* * *

Complete all of the above exercises before answering the following questions:

Would you say, on the basis of these activities, that writing within a given set of restrictions makes you feel less powerful?

Are you really less "free" when you write within given restrictions?

Are you more aware of the challenges of writing when you write freely or with restrictions?

Have any of your attitudes toward writing been changed by the activities on this page?

The Universe of Writing 6

Consider each of the following as an "opening" for a piece of writing:

(a) It was a brisk October morning....

(b) Baby carrots, shimmering with a golden glaze of soft buttery sweet sauce....

(c) Sometimes an idea burst into consciousness with the sudden illumination of a lamp in a cavern....

(d) I could feel the cold steel of the barrel against my naked back...

Examine your response to each of the "openings" above in the light of these questions:

Does your response show that you are capable of being triggered into action by a few words?

Have you found that you can be "inspired" by another writer's words?

Will your writing be any less your own when it is triggered or inspired by someone else's words?

* * *

Do any of the following have the power to charge or inspire you with the desire to express yourself in writing:

An old photograph of your parents or grandparents

A piece of music you know well enough to sing or hum

Dr. Martin Luther King's "I Have a Dream" speech

The development of face transplants

Can you find other sources with the power to charge and inspire you? Which ones have the greatest power?

Does it matter to you that other people are powerfully affected by things that don't affect you?

Will it be more important to you to respond to what moves you or to convey it to others? Will what moves you lose any of its power over you if you are unable to convey it to others?

* * *

Could you say, on the basis of the activities on this page, that the more powerful impulse toward writing is self-expression or communication?

Section III: The Enhancement of Writing

The Universe of Writing 7

Write a page or more on each of the following topics:

(a) A fictional story to "explain" how people came to wear clothes in the first place.

(b) The apparent reason why clothing of some kind has been adopted as a necessity in all cultures.

(c) How fashions in dress have changed during your lifetime.

(d) What the choice of clothes shows about a person.

(e) How "Nike" and "Adidas" trainers (or any two brands of the same type of clothing) are alike and not alike.

Examine your experience with the above in the light of these questions:

Did each of these topics demand that you proceed in the same way? If not, how did you adjust to the demands of each?

Would it be correct to say that one topic required you to use yourself as a scientist, another as a myth maker, another as a historian, etc.? If so, can you identify the kind of temperament you needed to adopt for each one?

Can you invent additional topics that are of the same essential kind as each one above, even though they are not concerned with clothing in any way? Can you find articles or books that correspond to each type?

Do any of these modes of writing require anything of you beyond the powers of common sense, observation, and questioning you employ every day of your life?

* * *

Can what you have done above help you to get started and work confidently on the following topics?

Compare and contrast the main characters in two situation comedies on TV.

How can a fool be identified?

Describe how a bicycle works.

How has the invention of the automobile influenced life?

The Universe of Writing 8

Experiment with some, or all, of the following "assignments" before considering the questions at the bottom of the page:

Describe a situation you "wouldn't be caught dead in" and explain how you talked your way out of it.

Supply a new set of words to the tune of a familiar song.

Write the first paragraph of a story. Give what you wrote to a friend to continue before taking it back and providing your own ending.

Provide an outrageous solution for a major social problem. The tone of your essay should be sober matter-of-fact.

Write a page in which everything you say is borrowed or quoted from others—books, people you know, TV programs, etc.

Write a page of advice so wise no one else can possibly understand you.

Write the truth about yourself—the truth that no one else knows.

Describe events in your own life in the style of a newspaper report.

> Can practice in writing lead one to become equally confident in one's powers as a writer and a speaker? More confident as a writer than as a speaker?
>
> Can writing become "second nature"?
>
> Can writing ever be intoxicating?
>
> Can writing combine joy and pain?
>
> Can one ever finish writing something convinced that it is a perfect expression of all that one is?
>
> Can one return to something one has written and be astonished at its quality? Its lack of quality?
>
> Can one catch oneself suddenly proofreading more carefully and feeling regret for the mistakes that have not been detected?
>
> Can one want others to respond, in writing, to what one has written?

The Universe of Writing 9

Conduct your own research in order to find answers to the following questions:

Which functions can writing perform better than speaking in business? In government? In religion? For oneself?

Was anything valuable lost when writing became so important in most cultures?

What would a society in which all knowledge is conveyed orally be like?

How would *your* life be affected if writing disappeared.

What would a society in which only a few people could write be like?

What special skills must people who cannot write develop when they live in a literate society?

Can you locate people in our society who live without writing? How has this affected their lives?

The Spirit of English

During most of the time I've been a teacher my employer has been a Department of English. For the first few years this bothered me. It bothered me because although I knew myself as a competent reader and writer, I didn't really feel that I knew "English." And every time a student asked me whether there was a rule about using conjunctions at the beginning of sentences, or whether I would please explain this entry in her grammar textbook or on the website. I hurriedly changed the subject. Explain something in a grammar textbook? Not likely, I could never understand it myself. The very thought of grammar textbooks—I too had bought one as a freshman and could never understand it—made me feel slightly faint. I guess I considered myself something of a fraud as a teacher of English. But after several years passed without anyone denouncing me publicly for impersonating an English teacher, my discomfort more or less faded away.

No doubt this feeling of unease and faint guilt had its roots in my secondary school experience. I had been something of a puzzle to my teachers: a boy who flunked every grammar test and yet was actually *interested* in writing and literature. In my school even the girls hesitated to admit they liked to write or ever read anything they weren't compelled to read.

When I recall how I felt in school I remember the conflict between two, seemingly irreconcilable, emotions. On the one hand I accepted the prevailing wisdom that someone who couldn't master the "mechanics" of grammar and spelling would never come to much. On the other hand, I knew perfectly well that I owned the English language and would someday become a writer. I know that English, as a living presence, was a part of me. I lived in it and it inhabited me. I had a feel for its words and the cadences of its sentences. My ears were so finely attuned to its melodies that the over-scrupulous correctness of a bookish foreign voice grated on my ear. The vowel sounds of other languages stuck in my throat and wouldn't come out. Finally, when I read a book by a foreign author, however excellently translated, I often found myself struck by an air of irreducible strangeness. Some quality of the writer's voice seemed rooted in his or her native language and a violation of my sense of the nature of things.

From my present vantage point I recognize that my teachers did not perceive that I arrived in their classrooms with an important job already done. I had prepared myself as every person does as part of his or her apprenticeship in a native language. That is, I had molded my flesh, so to speak, to the demands of functioning in English. I had made my hearing and my breathing and my voice embody the spirit of English. But since no deliberate attempt was made to link my sensitivities to what was taught as "English," I remained ignorant of how to apply what I knew of my native language to the study of grammar and mechanics.

Section III: The Enhancement of Writing

A few years ago, I came upon a chapter in one of Dr. Caleb Gattegno's books entitled *The Spirit of a Language*. This made me immediately aware that there was a way of approaching the content of the grammar books based on the enhancement of sensitivities rather than learning rules. It also led me to see that, in giving myself to the spirit of English, instead of another language. I have assimilated a certain way of breathing, thinking, and feeling.

This section contains exercises and activities that can perhaps help you to see to what extent you too have given yourself to the spirit to English; to see how you have molded your flesh and your mental climate in order to live through this language. The following pages may also help you to approach English grammar through disciplined, self-observation and without the need for a specialized vocabulary, explanations, or rules.

The Spirit of English 1

Do you know how you control the flow of air through your vocal apparatus to produce noises? You may have seen a diagram of this process, but do you know it from *inside*?

Gain an acquaintance with your vocal apparatus by monitoring what you do to produce sounds and variations of sound.

> Can you feel from within what you do with your abdomen? Which muscles in your throat and mouth are used?
>
> Are any of the sounds you can make coming from the same place? Are there any sounds that involve only your throat? Are there any sounds that require the use of your tongue, teeth, or lips? Your nose?
>
> What do you do to control the duration of a sound? Can all sounds be lengthened and shortened?

* * *

Practice using your vocal apparatus to make the widest possible range of sounds.

> Are all of the sounds you can make required for speaking English?
>
> Do you find any sounds that are not a part of English but that you recognize as belonging to another language?
>
> Do you find any sounds that are not, as far as your know, used in any language?
>
> Do you find any sounds that are used in English but not, as far as you know, in any other language?

Which sounds are easier to make—those associated with English or those you know from other languages? Which require a greater amount of energy to get them "right"? Why?

How quickly can you tell that a particular sound is a part of English? *Where* do you first know? In the muscles of your vocal apparatus? In your hearing?

* * *

See if it is possible for you to utter sequences of noises that feel and sound like English even though they contain no words of English. Also see if you can do the same thing in any other language you know.

> Does each language require you to breathe in a particular way?
>
> Do you find yourself making some sort of inner adjustment as you change from one language to another?

Section III: The Enhancement of Writing

Make each of the following statements TRUE or FALSE:

_____ 1. English has 26 sounds corresponding to the number of letters in its alphabet.

_____ 2. English has 6 vowel sounds.

_____ 3. English has "long vowels" and "short vowels." The former are made by stretching out the latter sounds.

_____ 4. The first sound in the word "pat" is like "puh."

_____ 5. Some syllables have 1 vowel sound in them, some more than one.

_____ 6. When we pronounce the word "possible" normally it has 2 beats (syllables).

_____ 7. When we pronounce the word "adding" normally we give it 2 beats and divide it into two bunches of sounds—ad-ding.

_____ 8. "Cough" is composed of 5 sounds, "thoughts" of 7.

_____ 9. Most of the time we say "the" and "a" and the first sound in "aloud" and "effective" as "long vowels."

_____ 10. Some consonantal sounds are longer than others, as English spelling suggests.

If you have marked any of these statements TRUE, listen to yourself more carefully.

> The following exercises are concerned with *sounds* not spelling. Try not to think about how the words look or which letters they contain.
>
> 1. Reverse the order of the sounds in these words. Tip, kiss, write, know, cull.
>
> 2. How many different English words can you make by inserting vowel sounds in the gaps: T__p, Sh__t, Kn__, K__t. (Remember, it is sounds which matter, not spellings.)
>
> 3. How many different words can you make by substituting another sound for one of the sounds in time, check, crank, cough.
>
> 4. What is the sound of the vowel in the second beat of each of these words: letter, different, interesting?
>
> 5. How many of the following words begin and end with the same sound: zoos, spellings, sounds, sides.

The following spontaneous writing sample was written by a woman who was referred to the Staten Island Community College Skills Center after she failed a grammar test during the second week of school:

> This is my first encounter with college life. The first week here was like eternal hell. There is just no other way to explain it.
>
> Every department and instructor wanted my Social Security number which I have never memorized. I think I've formed a mental block against knowing.
>
> I had dealings with the financial aid department who wanted to send me off campus to work, me a mother with two children. I was then sent to a woman who reminded me of Hitler. Her only concern was I work until five P.M. each day. She wasn't concerned with any personal problems ...

The spirit of English 2

Check to see how many different preparations of your vocal apparatus you need to make in order to utter each of the following words:

at, map, cough, interesting, anti-disestablishmentarianism

Do you know, from inside, how many distinct sounds there are in each of these words? Is this count confirmed by your hearing?

Do you know, from inside, how many beats there are in each one of these words? Is this count confirmed by your hearing?

Is it possible to isolate any of the sounds in any of these words without distorting them?

Are there any sounds that cannot be isolated without distortion?

Do you have any criteria, from inside, for knowing what is meant by "vowels," "consonants," and "syllables"?

* * *

Listen to yourself speaking each of the following words and then try to pronounce, in isolation, each of the vowel sounds. Be watchful to catch yourself when you change a sound in the act of isolating it.

at, up, it, pet, pot, girl, far, to, she, there, book, I, eight, owe, cow, oil, one

How many *different* vowel sounds have you found?

Can you identify, from inside, where each sound is made and what you do to make it come out clearly and distinctly?

Do any of the sounds come from closely adjacent places?

Is the difference between any pairs of similar sounds a function of the amount of breath required to say them?

Are there any sounds in this group that appear to be made by combining two sounds that are also said separately?

Can you find any additional vowel sounds in any of the sentences on this page that are commonly used in English but are not contained in the list above?

* * *

Read this particular sentence aloud carefully to yourself several times and listen to yourself as you read it.

How many beats are there in each of the words in the sentences?

Do all of the beats receive equal stress or are some beats "lighter" than others?

Can you identify the vowel sounds in the "lighter" beats? Are they clear and distinct sounds? Are these sounds common in English words of more than one beat?

The spirit of English 3

Listen to yourself speaking the following sentences in a normal manner:

> Are you going to go home or what?
>
> I said to him, "What do you mean?"
>
> The imperfections, serious as they appear now, will be greatly magnified by the time we come to market the product.

Count the number of pauses in each sentence, basing your count on what you hear.

> Are all of your pauses made for the same reason? Can you distinguish between those that allow you to catch your breath and those that are necessary to convey meaning?
>
> Are all the pauses of equal duration?
>
> Is there a pause between each successive pair of words as the conventions of printing suggest?
>
> Is there an average number of words between pauses? Check to find out.
>
> Are there any words that seem to be so closely linked to what follows that no pause is allowable?
>
> Are there any words that must be separated by pauses in order to make sense? By a pause before but not after? By a pause after but not before?

✻ ✻ ✻

Read the sentence above, changing the normal pattern so that a pause occurs after every second word.

> Are the sentences still "English"? Or are there only utterances composed of English words?
>
> Which contributes more to the sound of English—the words or the silence between words and phrases? Are you sure of your answer?

✻ ✻ ✻

Listen to yourself uttering the sentences above once more in a normal voice. Notice particularly which words and syllables in each sentence are stressed by your voice.

> Can you hear any relation between the stresses and the silences?
>
> When you stress a word or syllable, can you feel within you a sense of how soon the next pause will occur?

Section III: The Enhancement of Writing

Which of the following are "English":

_____ 1. Without blood is not living.

_____ 2. I disappeared it.

_____ 3. You cause that I am sad.

_____ 4. He had had that that she wants.

_____ 5. The nature is very beautiful.

_____ 6. Why you do that?

_____ 7. Why to me are you giving this?

_____ 8. The slithy toves were grying and gimbling in the wabes.

_____ 9. But out of the frying pan is he going into the fire.

_____ 10. Out of the flying pan into the friar.

Which of the following *could* be "English":

_____ 1. Fram de cram an hol mi glack.

_____ 2. Nroops gleet!

_____ 3. As eet tedwing?

_____ 4. Sfloan ar af Slgo?

_____ 5. Oofu ooflikoo ooftoo oofdontoo oofo?

The Spirit of English 4

Observe yourself when you are speaking to see whether you can hear, and feel from within, the "music" of English speech.

> Is there a beat underlying the melody of your words? (If you talk to yourself and tap with your feet, at the same time, the rhythm of your silent utterance, do you find that your speech has an underlying beat?) Is this an expression of your particular voice or English?

> Is there a tempo that is necessary to make your words "sound like English"? If you slow down or speed up your articulation of sounds, does it still sound right?

> Is there a melody you can detect in your own speech? Do other native speakers respect it also? Foreign speakers of English?

> Is there a characteristic pattern of intonation in what you say? What does your voice do at the beginnings and ends of statements? Can you detect whether what you do is unique to you or part of English?

* * *

Station yourself in a room where people are speaking a number of different languages simultaneously.

> Are you able to identify the speakers of English? Do you need to identify any of the words you hear in order to be sure?

* * *

Observe yourself when you are speaking to see if you can catch yourself moving your body while you talk. Are there any movements, however slight, in your shoulders, arms, or torso that are a part of speaking English?

Talk to yourself and try, at the same time, to exaggerate your bodily movements so that this dimension of your expression is fully visible.

> Do you know which of these movements are unique to you and which are a part of English? Observe others closely to find out.

* * *

Read the following so that they have the unmistakable sound of English:

1,038,276.

$26.82

$\sqrt[3]{8,926}$

$2,000 @ 28%

666,666,666,666.66

1.18768432323232

| 1 | 1 | & | 2 | 1 | 2 |
| R | U | 1 | 2 | ? | |

$$\frac{a^2 - 3(x-y)}{-2x}$$

763,480 lbs.

86" X 43'

3 gal. ~ 12 qts. ~ 24 pts.

* * *

Section III: The Enhancement of Writing

Compose 50-word telegrams using only those words that are essential to convey your basic meaning. Experiment to see how many of the words of normal speech can be omitted without sacrificing meaning.

Test the adequacy of your work by asking another native speaker of English to read your telegram(s) and reconstruct the meaning as it would be expressed in ordinary speech.

NOTE: In place of telegrams, the preceding exercises can be based on the kinds of "shorthand" employed in computer messaging and email communication.

The Spirit of English 5

Ask a friend to hum a few sentences at the speed of speech, making certain that as many of the components of talking as are compatible with this activity are represented in his/her performance.

> Do you have a "feel" for when sentences begin and end?
>
> Are you able to sense when a sentence is about to conclude? If so, how?
>
> Are you able to anticipate at the beginning whether a certain sentence will be long or short? If so, what tells you?
>
> Are you able to sense how many phrases a particular sentence contains? If so, what tells you?
>
> Are you able to sense how many words the speaker has in mind?
>
> Can you tell whether the speaker is making a statement or asking a question?

* * *

Listen to a friend, or a group of friends, talking informally. As they speak, tap twice with your pencil each time they come to the end of a sentence. Tap once when they leave a sentence unfinished and begin a new sentence.

> How do you know when to tap?
>
> Do you ever need to consciously analyze the grammar of what you hear?
>
> Would it be true to say that you have reliable aural criteria for English sentences? Are your criteria intellectual or somatic?

Continue listening, noting whether you sense a movement within you that is in sympathy with the flow of the speakers' words.

Do you have a "feel" for English sentences elsewhere within you besides in your ears?

The Spirit of English 6

Look quickly at the following:

When I _____ I _____ it.

Is it _____ or _____ ?

All of the _____ people were here.

Was a certain movement triggered in you when you perceived the above? How quickly?

Would you have responded differently if you had been *told* to "fill in the gaps"?

Look quickly at the following:

I _____ home.

I _____ to my home.

Did each gap in the above trigger an identical feeling? Or did you feel differently about each one, even though the amount of blank space was the same?

Does your sense of the width of the gap depend on the extent of blank space on the page or something within you?

Look quickly at the following:

Quand je _____ .

Whenever he _____ .

Did each of the blanks above trigger an identical feeling? Or did you sense a different inner movement in response to each one?

Did the amount of blank space seem sufficient to satisfy your inner sense of what would complete the sentences? Did you find yourself making verbal adjustments in order to cope with the amount of space allowed?

Did you feel yourself drawn to extend the statement beyond the limits of a single sentence?

Did this exercise trigger mostly words or the sense of a situation that might require such a choice of vocabulary? Did you feel any sense of a tone or atmosphere implicit in the given words?

What do you do within yourself when you are listening to someone speaking and their flow of words is broken in the middle of a sentence?

When I _____1._____ I _____2._____ it.

Is it _____3._____ or _____4._____ ?

All of the _____5._____ people were here.

Write in the number(s) of the gap(s) into which each of the words listed below would seem to fit.

sparsit _____   ak _____   cooka _____

kimbles _____   glater _____   ordled _____

lipiling _____   byfe _____   tisle _____

Count the number of *different* cues in each sentence that tell you *when* an action occurred, how many people were involved in it, and/or *where* it occurred:

Yesterday the two boys went together into the middle of the street.

Although I am feeling good now, I am being careful to watch myself.

The president hopes the congress will now approve his action in the next few days.

There, in the next room, is where they all ate their dinner today.

The Spirit of English 7

Ask a friend to read the following paragraphs to you (before you look at them yourself) at the speed of normal speech and without making any changes in the text. (They may need to practice in order to render the text properly.) As you listen, count the number of times you hear something that offends your ear.

1. The man wakes up. It was rain outside. He doesn wanna get up but he hadda. He gotted dress and made breakfasts. Then he's went to work.

2. She fell bad. Thing was very bore. She wish her father would understand how she's feel. He doesn't cared about her.

In listening to the passages, where did you need to focus your hearing in order to catch the location of the mistakes?

Were you attentive to the beginnings of words? The middles? The ends?

Did you listen to these passages as you would listen to any utterance in English?

* * *

Find out what happens when you speak without supplying enough air to fully enunciate the ends of your words.

Are you any less sure of what you want to say?

Are others able to understand you? Do they complain?

Do you ever do this in speech without noticing that you do it? Ask your friends.

* * *

Does speaking English demand that each and every word be enunciated clearly and fully in order to be understood?

Does writing allow you to function in the same way as when you speak?

Section III: The Enhancement of Writing

The Spirit of English 8

Do you ever catch yourself saying something you know is incorrect in English? If so, do you feel the need to correct yourself out loud? Silently? Do others notice? Do they correct you?

Do you ever catch yourself hesitating between two words or expressions, uncertain of which is correct English? If you do this, do others seem to notice?

Do you notice whether or not other people speak correct English? If you hear a mistake, do you correct the other person out loud? Silently?

Check you experience against that of others whom you know. Do all of you function in the same way?

Ask people who speak other languages if their experience is the same as yours both in English and in the other languages they know.

> Could you say, on the basis of this research, that the speakers of English care about correctness? Do they judge others on the correctness of their speech?

> Are the speakers of English more or less tolerant than the speakers of other languages?

When you write a personal letter, is it acceptable to your correspondent if you express yourself in the same words and sentence structure as when you speak? Or are you expected to write a language that is different from the one you speak?

Is it the same when you write a business letter? As essay for school? If there is a change, is it in vocabulary? The way sentences are formed?

Is the language of the newspaper very different from the way most intelligent people talk? Read portions of a newspaper aloud and listen to find out.

> Would you say, on the basis of this research, that acceptable written English is fairly close to common spoken English?

> Can you find out whether this is equally true of other languages?

* * *

Just Writing

1. Make sentences by using one word or expression from each column. Work from left-to-right, placing the words in the same sequence as the arrangements of columns. (You may omit column 3 if you wish).

2. Add additional words to the columns if possible and make additional sentences. (You may omit column 3 if you wish).

1	2	3	4	5	6	7	8	9
I	could	not	go	at	the	school		
The Italians	does		to walk	around	a	us		
Charles	might see			with				

3. Reverse the order of column 1 and 2 and make sentences.

4. Make sentences omitting 3.

5. Create a new column (#8) by writing in the words "if," "when," and "while" in the space provided. Then make sentences using the following orders:

    1 → 8 + 1 → 7[1]

    8 + 1 → + 1 → 7

6. Create a new column (#9) by writing in the words "and" and "but" in the space provided. Then make sentences:

    1 → 7, 9, 1 → 7

    8-9, 1 → 4, 9, 1 → 4 + 1 → 7

---

[1] Conventions: → = through (pick one from each column); + = and

Section III: The Enhancement of Writing

The Spirit of English 9

Draw a picture in the frame below:

Describe what you see in the picture.

Is there more than one acceptable way of phrasing what you see?

Can you write several descriptions (of approximately the same length) using a different choice of words and/or word orders in each one?

> Would you conclude, on the basis of this experiment, that English is a flexible or inflexible language?

✳ ✳ ✳

Compare the following drawings with the captions beneath them:

She opened a door in her bathrobe.

The book is by Mark Twain.

Is English a language that stresses precision or tolerates ambiguity? Are you sure of your answer?

* * *

Is anything indicated about the precision or ambiguousness of English by the number of ways in which words such as "this," "that," "one," and "it" can be used?

* * *

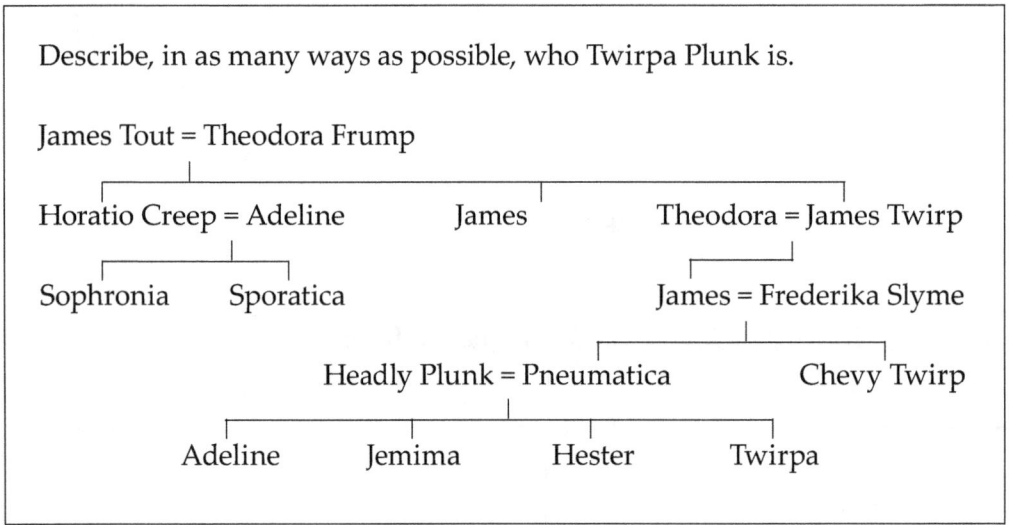

Describe, in as many ways as possible, who Twirpa Plunk is.

* * *

Are any of the following unacceptable as English sentences?
   I told him that that is not that interesting so that he shouldn't be surprised if that is turned down.

   Is it as it is?

   This one is O.K. but this one isn't as good as the ones here.

The Spirit of English 10

Do you have a "feel" for the difference between each of the expressions in the following pairs:

Look out the window!

Look out! The window!

going out for lunch

going out for baseball

drop out of school

drop out of the window

How many different expressions can you make by combining a word like "go" or "look" with words such as "at," "in," "on," etc.?

Is it characteristic of English to make combinations such as these?

Will you be able to check the meaning of such expressions by looking up each of the component words in a dictionary?

* * *

Draw a picture illustrating each of the following expressions:

    by the house
      around the house
        at the house
          through the house
        to the house
          from the house
            for the house

Does this exercise tell you everything about the role of "little words" in English?

* * *

Write a paragraph *without* using any "little words."

Is it indicative of the spirit of English that "little words" are used so commonly?

* * *

Create the maximum number of new words that may be formed by adding the following to other English words:
    -ty   -teen   -th

* * *

Make 100 words into negatives by adding a sound or a syllable.

* * *

List *all* the syllables that can be added to the beginning or end of English words to change the meaning.

The Spirit of English 11

Find opportunities in your own experience that provide evidence for considering the following questions:

Is English a language in which there are many resources for expressing politeness? Rudeness?

Is it a language that lends itself most easily to speaking softly or loudly?

Is it a language in which one can easily express tender emotions?

Is it a language in which philosophic statements generally seem to make sense?

Is it a language in which factual statements generally seem to make sense?

* * *

What happens when you use English to give traffic directions, describe a good meal, explain your feelings about someone, present a scientific definition? Does the language seem more suited to some of the above than to others? If so, which ones?

If you know another language, repeat the exercise and compare results.

* * *

For which of the following are there extensive vocabularies in English? Can any only be talked about using words imported into English from other languages?

Gardening

Food

Occult phenomena

Automotive parts

Literary Criticism

Finance

Mental health

Music

Engineering

Sociology

Does this exercise suggest anything to you about the spirit of English and those who speak English as a native language?

Section III: The Enhancement of Writing

The Spirit of English 12

Examine yourself as a speaker of English to determine answers to the following questions:

Is it consistent with the spirit of English for objects to be described and addressed as persons? Sometimes? Often? Seldom?

Is it consistent with the spirit of English for persons to be addressed or described as objects?

Are ideas or concepts described or addressed as persons?

Is it consistent with the spirit of English to categorize objects and ideas into "male" and "female" categories? Is it the same in other languages?

Is English precise about numbers of people? Does its grammar distinguish between more than one and more than two? Between a small group and a crowd? Is this reflected in the grammar of the language?

Is it more consistent with the spirit of English that the past is more important than the future? Is this reflected in the grammar of the language?

Is English very precise in distinguishing between wishing, wanting, hoping, and wondering?

Is English very precise in dealing with time? Can it distinguish clearly between happenings that occurred once and those that were habitual? Between what is happening now for the first time and what is continuing now from the past?

Do the following facts about the English language suggest anything about *you* and the way you perceive *your* experience?

"The past tense is used more in English than the future tense."

"English makes very little use of gender."

"English has no word for referring to a particular person without reference to his/her sex."

"In English many words referring to the nationality or ethnicity of persons are pejorative."

* * *

Just Writing

1. Make all the possible arrangements of two or more words that make sense:

can	am	rain	love
could	are	to rain	to love
may	be	raining	loving
might	been	rained	loved
must	had		
ought	has		
will	have		
would	was		
were			

2. Group the expressions you have made in pairs that indicate a clear contrast in meaning.

Section III: *The Enhancement of Writing*

The Spirit of English 13

Examine each of the following passages:

> And therefore, being uncertain whether my hap will be so good as ever to meet again with you, all ceremonies set aside in writing, I wish to you and my sister your own hearts' desire and also beseech you to make the same account of me which you do of any that you know you may most command. (From a personal letter written in 1566.)

> If I made myself intelligible yesterday, this letter will be expected; but expected or not, l know it will be read with candour and indulgence. You are all goodness, and I believe there will be need of even all of your goodness to allow for some parts of my past conduct. (From a personal letter written about 1815.)

Has the spirit of English changed since these letters were written?

Do you find anything in you that responds to these expressions from earlier times? Is there anything of the English *you* speak in them?

Have you noticed any changes in the language during your lifetime? If so, were these changes or modifications in the *spirit* of English?

Just Writing

Studying Words

I have mixed feelings about words. Although I am addicted to them and use them every chance I get, they have gotten me in a lot of trouble over the years, and I hate them.

At the precise moment when I am talking or writing, words generally leap into my consciousness and flow through my mouth or my hand without my thinking very much about them. Sometimes I am struck by the appropriateness (or inappropriateness) of some of the words that come to mind, but I've found that if I want to stay fluent, it doesn't help to scrutinize them too closely. In fact, if I'm very self-conscious about my vocabulary and try to choose each word carefully, I quickly find myself with nothing to say.

As soon as I have *finished* saying what I wanted to say, however, the words suddenly become terribly important. People are always reminding me that I really said this or that and wanting to know how I could say such-and-such now when I said such-and-such else yesterday. And if I put something I've written away for a couple of days and look at it again, most of what I thought I was saying has disappeared. All that's left is a bunch of words.

I've also discovered that I live in a society dominated by verbiage and one in which the rumble of words often has greater reality than that to which the words are presumed to refer. Like Chateaubriand, I often find myself wondering if "language was given to humankind in order that they might disguise their thoughts." Further, I recognize that throughout my education the primary emphasis was upon mastering the specialized vocabularies of each discipline. Whether or not I learned how to function as a grammarian, chemist, geometer, or artist, I always learned how to talk like one! Looking around me at newspapers and politicians and television and street corner loungers, I often conclude that words are everything; that nothing else exists except the word. Still, I know within me that this is absurd. Most of my inner experience is conducted independently of words and even of language. Emotions are not words. Feelings are not words. Thoughts are often wordless.

Perhaps things would be different if our ancestors had invented a method of writing in which more of the components of language were encoded simultaneously, as in musical notation. But the fact is that they chose to create a code covering only the words. For this reason, I suppose, the study of language has always been largely confined to observing the behavior of words.

An immense literature has been generated to describe how words behave. No one person could possibly survey all that the grammarians, linguists, and philologists have written. Still, there is a more pedestrian study of words that can be of interest to those of us who are not specialists: to observe what uses of words we make in our lives. What I have tried to provide in the following few pages are some entries into the study of words that are compatible with our needs as daily users of language.

Studying Words 1

Reflect on the following statements, asking yourself at the same time what they tell you about the nature of words and yourself as a user of words.

- Words are noises.
- Words are arbitrary noises.
- Words have meaning only because we give them meaning.
- Each of us has lived without words as a baby.
- Perception and action preceded words.
- Imagery preceded words.
- Our sense of truth preceded words.
- We retain many ways of knowing that are independent of words.
- Each of us constructed a personal universe of meanings before entering the universe of words.
- We attached some of our meanings to noises supplied by the environment.
- We heard noises in the environment for which we had no meanings.
- We uttered noises we had endowed with meaning and noises that were meaningless.
- We remain, all of our lives, both inside and outside the universe of words.
- Most of our words are not invented by us but borrowed.
- We endow a common and public vocabulary with our own unique and private meanings.
- Words provide a link between what is unique in our personal universe of meanings and what we can share with others.
- In using words we give up some of our independence.

Studying Words 2

Reflect on the following statements, asking yourself at the same time what they tell you about the nature of words and yourself as a user of words.

- o Words are the common possession of many and must meet the needs of each.
- o Each word is a label for any member of a class of meanings that are usually associated.
- o No word has only one, unique, and fully specific meaning.
- o Words are always ambiguous.
- o Words are "defined" by reference to other words.
- o Definition compounds the ambiguity of words.
- o Words convey an awareness of selected atoms of experience, extracted from the whole.
- o Words are an analytic tool—a way of breaking down the whole in order to focus on a part.
- o Words are always abstract.

What does this picture show?

Section III: The Enhancement of Writing

Studying Words 3

Reflect on the following statements, testing them against the experience of your own life.

> That because we endow them with meaning, words have the power to trigger changes in our inner state.
>
> That almost any word in our own language has been granted this power.
>
> That we may grant to certain words the power to mobilize vast amounts of energy through our emotions and outward behavior.
>
> That we may invest our energy in certain words to the extent that they dominate our entire life.
>
> That we may live through certain words to the extent that we neglect our sense of truth, our perceptions, etc., etc.
>
> That we can endow words with "reality" and suppose that only what we have already labeled exists.
>
> That we can suppose that the actuality of others is completely defined by the words they utter or the words we apply to them.
>
> That we can assume the universe of words is the *only* universe we inhabit.

---

you are a hypocrite whoever you are!

Technophobe   Christian   Art   Sexism

Sticks and stones can break my bones but words can never hurt me?

Studying Words 4

Observe yourself for the briefest moment of which you are capable. How adequate are words as a medium for rendering this experience?

> Are the words that are triggered expressive of the texture of your experience as you felt if from within?

> How many words would be needed to convey your awareness during this moment?

> Do you have a vocabulary adequate to render the outward circumstances surrounding this moment? The inner dynamics?

Attempt to write something expressing the texture of another moment immediately after it occurs.

> Were you successful in satisfying yourself?

> Was what you wrote "true" to the moment?

> Could you feel the pressure of your words distorting your experience?

***

Take whatever you wrote in the previous exercise and hold it to your ear.

> Can you hear the words?

> Are *written* words noises?

Look at your text and "read" it (silently).

> What is triggered by the marks on the page? Noises? Meanings? Are you sure of your answer?

Studying Words 5

Reflect on the meaning of the following statement, asking yourself whether they reveal anything new to you about the medium of words.

Words may be added to other words, producing sequential combinations called "expressions," "phrases," "sentences," etc.

Words may be inserted or extracted from within existing sequences, producing modifications of the original meaning.

Words with similar meanings may be substituted for one another, producing equivalent expressions.

The sequential arrangement of words may be varied, producing alternative versions of sense or nonsense.

Non-equivalent words may be substituted for one another, producing metaphors.

Words may be used to trigger other words, producing specialized combinations such as "synonyms," "opposites," and "associations."

Experiment to see what you can do with words by adding, substituting, inserting, and extracting according to the descriptions given above.

Would you conclude, on the basis of this experiment, that there is an "algebra" of words?

Is this "algebra" something you have practiced before doing this exercise?

Do you know more of this "algebra" than is conveyed on this page?

How complex is this "algebra"? Is it simpler or more complicated than the algebra you studied in school?

* * *

Write a meaningful sentence of at least 40 words.

Divide your 40-word sentence into at least 4 separate sentences. (Words may be added if necessary.)

Recombine your sentences into one sentence that is different from the original sentence.

Studying Words 6

Can you find examples of words that function as labels for *things*? For *actions*? For *states of being*?

Is there a clear distinction in vocabulary between these functions?

* * *

Can you find examples of words that function to express qualities and attributes we perceive through our senses?

Is there a clear distinction in vocabulary between those words that express the qualities and attributes of things and those that express actions or states of being?

* * *

Can you find examples of words that function to express relationship in space and time?

* * *

Can you find examples of words that function to help us overcome this difficulty: although the units of speech are strung together one-at-a-time, everything can happen simultaneously in real life?

* * *

Can you find examples of words that function to save time and energy by substitution for other words that are labels for things or people?

* * *

Can you find examples of particular words that can fulfill two or more of these functions?

* * *

Can you find examples of particular words that can fulfill two or more of these functions if they are changed slightly?

* * *

Can you find examples of particular words that can only function in one of these ways?

* * *

Can you determine which classes of words above are most numerous? Least numerous?

Section III: The Enhancement of Writing

> his, me, he, I, your, she

1. Fill in the blanks with words from the box:

    _____ was told to give _____ money to _____.

2. Put each of the words you have used at the top of a column. Then add all the words you can think of that belong in each column.

    (a)   (b)   (c)

    Do you know why 3 columns are needed?

> of, an, in, to, for, by, from

1. Fill in the gaps with words from the box:

    I can go_____New York_____Chicago_____train or_____a car or_____a bus.

    The TV is _____the table_____the door _____ the bedroom.

2. Fill the box up with other words that belong there.

1. Fill in the gaps:

    I like _____people but I dislike _____people.

    If you go to _____Algeria you can see the _____Sahara.

2. Fill the box with other words like those you put in the gaps.

Studying Words 7

What have we done to certain of our words to make them express our awareness that whatever we perceive or do happens in time?

* * *

What have we done with words to express our awareness that perceptions and actions may exist as wishes or unfulfilled possibilities as well as actualities?

* * *

How have we organized our words to express our awareness that present, past, and future coexist?

* * *

How does our use of words such as I, you, he, she, etc. express our awareness of relativity as a fact of life?

* * *

How does the fact that we can say "I" or "me" express our awareness that we can act and be acted upon?

* * *

How do words such as quickly, eagerly, slowly, etc. express our awareness that each of us has a will?

Section III: The Enhancement of Writing

> I _____ to school at 8:00 in the morning. As I _____ down the hall to my classroom I _____ a man _____ toward me. As he _____ closer to me I _____ that he _____ my friend Richard.
>
> 1. Fill in the gaps to make a story about something that has happened.
> 2. Fill in the gaps so that the story is happening now.
> 3. Fill in the gaps so that the story is about something that could happen.
> 4. Fill in the gaps so that the story expresses a wish.

* * *

Who does Robin have in mind when he speaks to Alice and says "him"?

If he says "you," can he be referring to Edward?

Does Edward have the same "he" in mind when he speaks to Alice?

If Alice, Robin, or Edward says "me," do they refer to the same person?

Why is none of this confusing?

Studying Words 8

Can you find specific examples of each of the following?

Words it is easy to begin sentences with.

Words it is impossible to begin sentences with.

Words it is easy to end sentences with.

Words that seldom, if ever, end sentences.

Words that come in the middle of sentences but seldom at the beginning or end.

Words that make sense after "I."

Words that never make sense after "I."

Words that make sense after "the."

Words that never make sense after "the."

Words that make it possible to combine two sentences into one, or three into one, or four into one.

Words that make it possible to prolong sentences by adding another part on the end.

Words that make it possible to stretch sentences by inserting a part in the middle.

Words that can be added at the beginning to make sure that a sentence will be long.

Words that can easily follow other words that end in __ly.

Words that can easily precede words ending in _____ly.

Words that can be found scattered throughout sentences.

Words that are always found in the same place in sentences.

Words that change their meaning as their location in the sentence changes.

Words that retain the same meaning, although their location can be changed.

Section III: The Enhancement of Writing

Fill in the gaps:

However, _____ if _____
Originally _____
_____. _____ only if _____
or if _____ but _____. In other words, if
_____. After all, _____
_____. In the final analysis _____.

At the *beginning* of the ⟦modern⟧ age the ⟦atomic⟧ *concept* was linked closely with that of ⟦chemical⟧ *elements*.

1. Substitute another word for each of those in italics. You may change the meaning if you like, but the sentence must still make sense.

2. Substitute words for those in boxes. You may change the meaning, but the sentence must still make sense.

3. Substitute words for all those that have not already been changed.

Studying Words 9

Examine the table below and see if you can find additional words to place in each column.

1	2
psychological	psychology
fishy	fish
analytical	analysis
yellow	yellow

3	4
psychologize	psychologically
fish	fishily
analyze	analytically
yellowed	yellow

Can you find any words that could be placed in each of the columns without any change? With a small change?

Can you find any words that will fit into one or more columns but not into every column, even with a change?

Can every word of English be added to at least one of these columns? Or would more columns be needed? If so, how many more columns?

Which column(s) contains words with which it is easy to begin sentences?

Which column(s) contains words that normally follow words such as those in Column 1? Column 2? Column 3? Column 4?

Which columns are potentially the most lengthy? The shortest?

Can any column(s) be used to form one-word sentences that are acceptable as "correct"?

Has this exercise shown you anything *new* about the way English words behave? About what you know of the language?

Section III: The Enhancement of Writing

Place words in the circles and at the ends of the arrows as indicated:

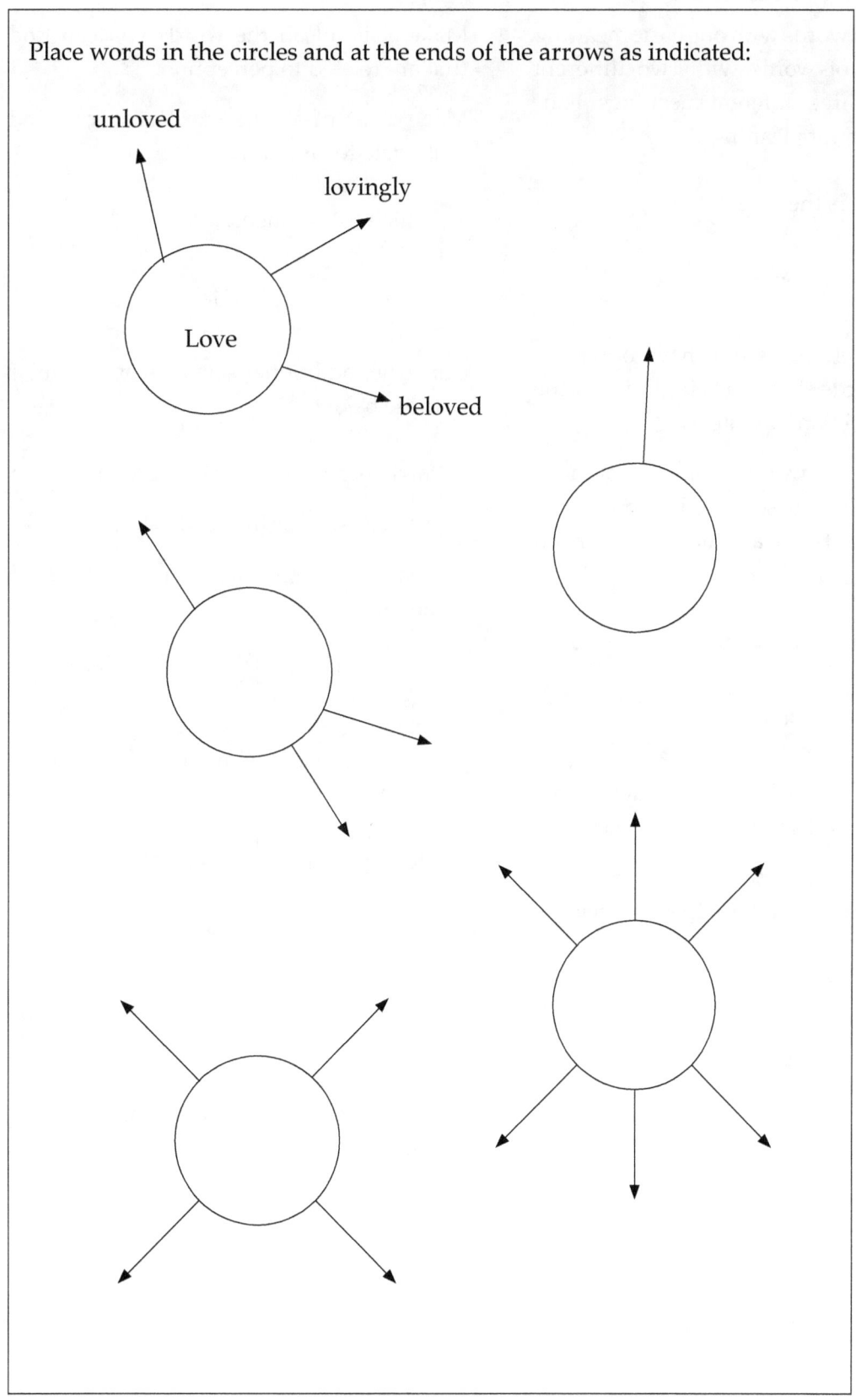

Studying Words 10

Make a list of words with one basic meaning. Make a list of words with two different meanings. Three different meanings. Four or more different meanings.

Which list is the longest?

* * *

Make a list of words that have opposites. Do these words show any similarity in the way they function in sentences?

Make a list of words that do not have opposites. Do these words show any similarity in the way they function in sentences?

Which list is the longer?

* * *

Make a list of words that have few synonyms. Do they function similarly in sentences?

Make a list of words with many synonyms. Do they function similarly in sentences?

Which list is the longer?

* * *

Make a list of all the words you can find that are related to perception.

Make a list of all the words you can find that relate to emotions.

Which list is longer?

* * *

Construct additional sets of words similar to those below:

    terrible, poor, fair, good, excellent, superb

    least, less, some, more, most

    penny, nickel, dime, quarter, half-dollar, dollar

* * *

Invent expressions similar in form to the following:

    Her eyes blazed and her voice exploded.

* * *

Invent expressions similar in form to the following:

    His face was pale as putty, and his hands shook like a TV antenna in a wind storm.

* * *

Section III: *The Enhancement of Writing*

Invent expressions to convey the following as vividly as possible:

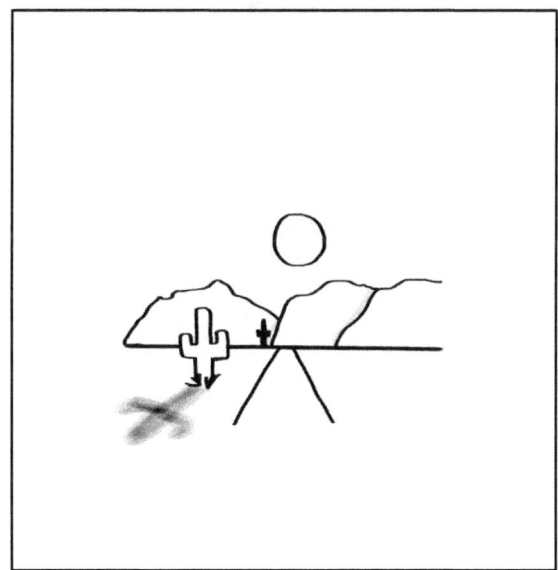

Studying Words 11

Construct a diagram such as the one below and place a word, chosen at random, in the circle. At the end of each arrow, write in another word that is triggered in your mind by the word in the circle. Continue to supply additional arrows and words as long as you can. Then use each of the words in the "cluster" as the basis for triggering a new cluster.

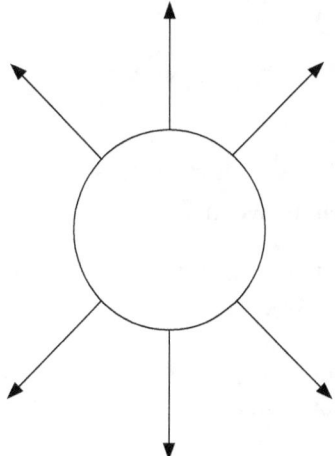

Could you say, on the basis of this exercise, that there is any word without the power to trigger other words?

Are some words more "powerful" than other words?

What makes a word "powerful"?

* * *

Studying Words 12

Do you know yourself as someone who has invested emotionally in words?

Are there certain words that can make you angry? Sad? Happy? Which are they?

Do you know what you have done within yourself to endow these noises with the power they now have? Can you identify the energy in you that is mobilized by the impacts of these noises?

* * *

Do you know yourself as someone who is vulnerable to words?

Are you ever conscious of feeling an affinity for certain words?

Does something get triggered in your inner climate whenever these "special" words are heard? Uttered?

Have you noticed yourself choosing to use certain words because you have a "feel" for them? Do you ever choose words for which you have a "feel" even though you are uncertain about their precise meaning?

* * *

On paper or on a screen, list some words that feel good as they roll off your tongue.

Do you ever catch yourself being betrayed by your own words?

* * *

Do you ever catch yourself deliberately choosing words in order to disguise your thoughts?

* * *

Do you ever catch yourself substituting words for understanding?

* * *

Do you ever catch yourself retaining words while losing grasp of their meaning?

* * *

Do you ever catch yourself using words as a filter for experience?

* * *

Do you ever catch yourself using your vocabulary as an instrument for perceiving the present in terms of your past?

Section IV:
Research Activities for Teachers of Writing

This section of the book is reserved for the reader who wishes to make a thorough and detailed study of writing through the discipline of observing himself or herself as well as others engaged in the process of composing.

The exercises and activities and experiments contained in these chapters are particularly challenging to me because they are "open-ended." I consider them not so much as questions to be answered as invitations to pursue research into the most mysterious aspect of writing—what happens in the writer's mind.

Just Writing

Investigating the Invisible Parts of Writing

More than two hundred years ago, a captive African on a slave ship studied the mysterious relation between the ship's captain and his books:

> "I had often seen my master employed in reading and I had a great curiosity to talk to the books as I thought they did....for that purpose I have often taken up a book and have talked to it and then put my ears to it, when alone, in hope it would answer me; and I have been very much concerned when I found it remained silent." *Interesting Narrative of Olaudah Equiano* (1789).

Since I first came upon this passage, it has remained with me as a constant reminder of how mysterious reading and writing are; mysterious because so much is hidden, so little is visible at the surface. Equiano's insight was a simple one, anyone might have grasped and articulated it, but encountering it in his book made me aware that I had missed something fundamental in my own study of literacy. I had neglected the "invisible" parts of writing, the inner movements that make the visible act of composition comprehensible.

What do we do within ourselves to make writing "talk" for us and to us? These are questions that have not been extensively explored by most of us, although some vague guideposts have been provided by those who have spoken of "inspiration" and "the process of creation."

When, as an Equiano's day, literacy was the carefully guarded possession of an elite, it was inevitable that it should be endowed with impenetrable mystery and an air of sanctity. But in an age such as our own, when universal literacy is a cherished ideal, it is less acceptable that so little effort should be made to probe the mystery. We want everyone to learn to write and yet we have failed to invent adequate tools for studying the invisible parts of writing—what goes on in our minds during the process of composition.

It seems to me that study of the invisible parts of writing requires that we develop new sensitivities. We need to find ways of enhancing certain mental processes so swift and fugitive that their existence often passes unnoticed. More specifically we need to focus our attention on questions such as the following:

> Can we make ourselves so vulnerable to our inner dynamics that we have direct experience of the generation and movements of our thoughts?

> Can we find mental exercises for the purpose of observing the process by which thoughts are transformed into language?

> Is "inspiration" an esoteric experience, reserved for only a few chosen souls,

or is it something we all experience as a component of finding something to say?

What is this thing we call our "voice," and how does it mediate between our thoughts, which are inner movements of ourselves, and language, which is common and public?

How much of language is verbal and how much is a matter of nonverbal vocal components?

How do we manage to coordinate the processes of generating language, which is very swift, and of transcribing words, which is much slower?

Some of these questions have already been touched upon in earlier sections of this book, but only very superficially. The pages in this section have been prepared with the aim of penetrating further—although perhaps only a little further—into the invisible parts of writing.

Investigating the Invisible 1

Sit quietly for a few moments without focusing your consciousness on anything.

> Was there any moment when your mind was totally empty? When you were unaware of the presence of words? Thoughts? Emotional stirrings? Perceptions? Images?
>
> Were there moments when your mind was relatively empty? If so, was this because you had ceased summoning thoughts and feelings or because you were rejecting or suppressing those that came?
>
> Was there ever a moment of which it would be true to say that you were aware of nothing within you that might be expressed in some way? (No sensations, fears, thoughts, etc.)
>
> Can you say, on the basis of this experiment, that your mind is ever a total blank?

* * *

Sit quietly for a few minutes, with your eyes closed, in a room that is still.

> Was there any moment when thoughts and feelings were not triggered from within or without?
>
> Was there any moment when you suddenly became aware that an image had been triggered from within you? Were other images evoked by the first one?

* * *

Sit quietly for a while, with your eyes closed, in a room that is still. After several minutes, turn on a radio and try to catch whatever happens within you during the first moment.

> Were you conscious of the impact of an energy upon you when the radio was turned on? Could you feel yourself being struck?
>
> At the moment when the sound of the radio reached you, were you aware of inner movements being triggered by this influx of energy?
>
> Were you aware that you had something new to express within yourself, that new feelings and images had been evoked, by this impact?
>
> Could you say that your breathing was changed, however slightly, in response to the impact? Would it be true to describe such a change as "an inspiration"?

Section IV: For Teachers of Writing

Investigating the Invisible 2

Focus your attention on an object near to you at this moment.

Do you only see what would be visible to a camera focused on the same spot.

Are you aware of the simultaneous presence of images triggered by what is before you and inner images you have evoked in response to what is there?

Is what you see in this moment unaffected by your memory? Your emotional state? Your prejudices?

Are any of your images related to what is before you by similarity? Contrast?

Do you catch yourself changing what is before you so that it can be mixed with the contents of your mind to produce images in which past and present are fused?

* * *

Look at the following picture and determine what you see.

Was there a moment when you had a simultaneous perception of the picture you first saw and the picture evoked by the title?

Is it characteristic of you to perceive your experience in several frames of reference at once?

Is your perception usually a matter of making simple representations of what is before you? Or do you often become aware of many different images and feelings at once?

Would it be true to say, on the basis of this and other experiences, that you relate to whatever can be perceived in a very complex way?

When you use language to supply labels for your perceptions, do you take into account the complexity of what you do when you perceive?

Does the quality of your perceptions often require that you express your experience in terms of metaphors?

The title of the picture is "A Bear Climbing a Tree."

Investigating the Invisible 3

Spend some time observing your inner climate or state just before and during writing.

> Can you catch the presence of a certain climate that signals to you that you can find something to say? Is this climate localized in any particular place?

> Can you catch the presence or a particular feeling that signals the arrival of inhibitions? Is it localized in any particular place(s)?

> Can you catch any movement of energy within you as images and words are generated? Do you feel physically expanded or contracted during this process? Focus on your abdomen and chest cavity to find out.

> Are you ever aware of the simultaneous presence of feelings of inhibition and release as you write? Can you detect changes in the balance between these feelings?

* * *

Practice monitoring your inner climate when you are speaking, writing, or engaged in other activities.

> Is there a particular climate or state that signals to you that you have made contact with a "meaning" that is not yet present as imagery or language? Can this feeling be localized?

> Is there ever a moment—of whatever duration—when "meaning" is experienced only as a mobilization of energy within you? Have you caught the quality of such moments?

> Is there ever a moment when you experience your "meaning" as no more than an image? Have you caught and held the quality of such moments without giving word to them?

> Is there ever a moment when you experience "meaning" generating language? Does this involve a mobilization of energy beyond what there was to make contact with the meaning?

> Is there ever a moment when meaning and language are held together in suspension, so to speak, to see whether the words that were evoked are compatible with the meanings?

> Does it ever happen that you are unable to find language—when your contact with meaning does not evoke language with which it is compatible? Can you discriminate, on the level of energy changes within you, when you have mobilized yourself to make contact with a meaning but not to evoke words?

Investigating the Invisible 4

The questions given below may help you to identify for the purposes of study some of the components of "thinking about what to write." Such study will only be possible if you are sufficiently watchful to catch yourself during the moments when you are actually engaged in the activity under examination.

> What does it mean to say, "Now I see what I want to say"? Does mental imagery often play a role in evoking something to write about? If so, how considerable a role? Is all imagery necessarily *visual*? If there are other kinds, what are they?

> How dynamic is the experience of "thinking about what to write"? Is it ever really possible to be completely focused on one thing at a time? Is there ever a moment when you are not actively selecting among your feelings, images, thoughts, words, etc.? Is there ever a moment when you are not stressing some and ignoring others?

> Once words enter into your process of composition, is it possible to maintain the integrity of whatever thoughts may have preceded words? Does the presence of words lead to a modification of what went before? What happens to those thoughts and dimensions of thoughts that are not expressible in language? Does the presence of words trigger other words? And further images, feelings, etc.?

> Does one ever operate without "second thoughts" intervening at every moment? Does mental composing ever occur in the absence of mental editing?

Investigating the Invisible 5

Experiment to see if you can slow down your process of composing by writing in a foreign language or writing backwards.
Do you find that you can be more aware of what you are doing when you compose in this way?

> Do you find that you are more aware of where you place your conscious attention?

> Does it make sense to say that, during the process of writing, your consciousness is continually being focused and refocused in different parts of you? Can you catch the moments when you are "*in* your imagery," "*in* your voice," "*in* your ear," or "*in* your hand"?

* * *

Do you know, on the basis of self-observation, that you use your voice as an instrument in composing?

* * *

Do you know, on the basis of self-observation, whether you use your ear as an instrument for monitoring your composing?

* * *

Do you know, on the basis of self-observation, whether you use your hand as an instrument for abstracting words from speech?

* * *

Can you say, on the basis of self-observation, that your inner activity of writing requires deliberate, continuous, shifts of consciousness among several mental instruments that function together to produce the outward behavior called "writing"?

Investigating the Invisible 6

Was there a time in your life when you used your voice but not language?

Is this still true when you cry? Strain to grasp a word that escapes you? Feel for the right expression in a foreign language? Are struck speechless?

✻ ✻ ✻

When you speak, which more completely expresses you—the language you use or your voice?

Which is closer to your inner dynamics—your vocabulary or your voice?

At the moment when you are thinking of something to say, which comes first—the awareness that you can "give voice" to something or the words you will utter? If you are not sure, experiment to find out.

✻ ✻ ✻

Is it necessary to actually utter sounds aloud in order to be aware of the functioning of your voice?

Do you know, on the basis of self-observation, that you maintain an "inner voice"? Are you attentive to its functioning?

✻ ✻ ✻

Section IV: For Teachers of Writing

Investigating the Invisible 7

Do you know, on the basis of self-observation, what your voice contributes to speaking in addition to articulating the words and structures that belong to the language?

Does intonation come from your language or from you?

Does phrasing come from your language or from you?

Do the silences in each statement come from the language or from you?

Observe yourself when you are speaking and see whether you can make any progress in answering the following questions:

Can you say that the energy mobilized by your voice is heard from outside but felt inside?

Can you feel your voice reverberating inside you? When you speak aloud? When you talk to yourself? Can you localize the reverberations?

Do the internal reverberations of your voice strike chords that are in sympathy with other currents of feeling within you?

Is what you have discovered about speaking also true of writing?

* * *

Try to make yourself vulnerable to the internal reverberations of your voice, both when you are speaking aloud and when you use "inner speech" (if you do use it).

Can you feel the presence of a "tone" or "tune" underlying each utterance?

Can individual words be altered or omitted without affecting the tune?

When do you establish contact with the tune? Before the words come? At the same time?

Is it possible to establish contact with the tune and maintain that contact without applying words to it?

Which seems closer to the meaning you wish to express—your words or the tune?

* * *

Ask someone to interrupt you several times while you are speaking.

Do you find that your consciousness of the tune remains with you during the moments when you are unable to summon or utter words?

* * *

Experiment to see whether you can interrupt yourself when you are speaking and then continue by uttering the tune of your statement without thinking about the words.

Can you express what you want to say by uttering that tune of an intended statement much faster than you normally speak and without giving conscious thought to the words?

If you resume speaking in a normal manner, do you find that there is a quality in them, at the level of sound, that is compatible with the tune of your expression? Do they seem chosen as if to "fit" an underlying music that preceded them?

Investigating the Invisible 8

Compose a letter to a friend out loud, deliberately choosing each of your words one-at-a-time.

Are you able, working in this way, to maintain contact with the meaning you started with?

Is focusing so intently on words *per se* compatible with facility in composing?

* * *

Compose a letter to a friend, out loud, at the speed of normal speech—or as close to that speed as possible.

Do you find that you are very much concerned with words *per se* in order to find the expressive resources you need?

Do you "think of the words" or are they more or less spontaneously triggered into your consciousness as you require them?

Are the words seemingly triggered by an "inner dictionary" or the presence within you of your subject? Is your imagery at work in triggering words?

* * *

Compose, out loud, on a subject you know very little about.

Do words come easily?

If there is a decrease in facility, is it because you lack vocabulary, or is it the absence of something else?

Investigating the Invisible 9

Place yourself in a situation where there is so much noise that you literally cannot hear yourself speak.

> Are you equally unable to hear yourself from within?

Must you utter a statement aloud in order for it to be monitored by your system of hearing? Have you experimented to find out?

Is "hearing" a function only of your somatic ear? Is there an inner component that is also capable of hearing?

Do you know, on the basis of self-observation, which instrument informs you whether a particular utterance "makes sense," is grammatically "correct," "sounds right"?

* * *

When you use your systems for sound production and hearing in speech, do you have direct, somatic knowledge of words? Or is the awareness of words *per se* imposed on speech by your intellect? If you are not sure, compare the experience of listening to people speaking in a variety of languages including some you know and some that are foreign to you.

* * *

Experiment to see whether when you write, your hearing is focused on words or the intervals into which the words fit.

> When you catch yourself in a mistake, do you know what it is that "sounds wrong"? is it the word(s)? The place the word occupies?

Investigating the Invisible 10

Do you know what is happening in the muscles of your hand at the moment when words appear on paper?

> Is your hand functioning as a mechanical instrument?
>
> Is your hand in any sense a center of consciousness? Can you catch yourself putting your awareness there?
>
> Does it make any sense to say that your hand "knows" what it is doing? Is its action merely an automatism?

* * *

Experiment to see if you can put some of your consciousness *in* your hand while you are actually engaged in writing.

> Is there any expressive "feel" in your hand as there is in your voice? Does your hand maintain any contact with the sound of what you write?
>
> Is there any "feel" in your hand for the non-vocal components of speech such as intonation, melody, and rhythm?
>
> Is there any "feel" in your hand for the resonance of particular words? Does it resist some and surrender to others?
>
> Is there any "feel" in your hand for the shapes of words? If so, is this anything resembling an imagery?

* * *

Utter a long statement aloud and then transcribe it.

> At the moment when you began to write, were any of the words already held in your hand?

> Where were the remaining words of the statement held as you were transcribing them? In your hand? In your ear? In your voice? Are you sure of your answer?

> If you omitted any words (or parts of words) while you were transcribing, where did you feel the awareness that something had been lost? In your hand? In your verbal memory? Both? Are you sure of your answer?

Investigating the Invisible 11

Has pursuing any of the questions in this section enhanced your awareness of invisible parts of writing of which you were already familiar?

❋ ❋ ❋

Have any of the questions or exercises expanded your awareness of the invisible parts of writing?

❋ ❋ ❋

Have you gone beyond what was suggested by the questions and exercise? Have you engaged in original research beyond the scope of these few pages?

Section IV: For Teachers of Writing

Studying Writers in the Classroom

For many years I believed that writers were a special breed of people whose work was accessible only in a library or a bookstore. It didn't strike me as curious that for every hour I spent with such authors, I consumed many more in reading what my students had written. In other words, I was surrounded by writers every day of my working life and I didn't even notice it!

I now recognize that, for better or worse, the authors I have the best opportunity to spend time with are my own students. In fact, these are the *only* writers (other than myself) I am ever likely to examine carefully, at close range, for they allow me certain liberties that no "professional" will ever permit.

My students let me watch them when they are actually composing and editing. I am able to ask them questions about their experience while it is still fresh. It is possible for me to read what they have written with some knowledge of how it was produced. Is it conceivable that any established author would allow me to do likewise?

Anyone who teaches composition can receive the gift of his or her students' experiences as writers—but only if he or she has the wisdom to ask for it. The truth eluded me during the many years when I encouraged my students to do all their writing at home; offstage, so to speak. Reading papers without access to the authors' processes of composing and editing taught me nothing about writing. If anything, it confirmed the prejudices and preconceptions with which I began.

The pages that follow are intended to suggest what can be learned by using the classroom as laboratory for the study of active, living writers.

Note: All of the above was written during the 1970s, when all of my teaching took place in a physical classroom, where I had abundant opportunities to observe my students writing and question them before and after about their experience. This situation continued more or less unchanged as the site of instruction shifted from a traditional classroom to a computer lab or classroom during the mid 1980s. However, it changed dramatically when classes went fully online during the late 1990s. Since that time, all of the students' writing activity occurs "off-stage," with the result that it is often difficult to find out what combination of inner awarenesses and outward behaviors have created a specific written product.

At present (2018) I sometimes need to use the telephone, email, and/or video conferencing software to observe and question students in order to penetrate the mystery behind their work. However, it still remains the case that what appears as the product of writing activity on paper or a screen is a very unreliable guide to the process that created it, especially those parts of the process that cannot be traced through outward observation, analysis of key strokes, etc. The most essential aspects remain where only the writer can locate them!

Studying Writers 1

Given a piece of written work to read and interpret, could a careful examination of the text (unconfirmed by any other evidence) allow you to answer any of following questions with certainty?

Who actually composed this? Does it represent the labor of a single author or a committee?

Is it a first draft or the product of successive revisions?

Is it an original manuscript or a copy?

Has it been proofread by its author and/or anyone else?

Are any errors it contains the result of carelessness? Ignorance?

Is it legitimate to draw any inference about an author or his/her writing ability without definitive answers to the preceding questions?

* * *

Given a writing sample, taken under controlled conditions, could a careful examination of the text (unconfirmed by any other evidence) allow you to answer any of the following questions with certainty?

Is the writer concerned with saying something and/or with avoiding errors?

Is the writer employing *all* his/her resources as a speaker of English or is he/she deliberately restricting vocabulary and syntax in order to avoid mistakes in spelling, usage, etc.?

Has the writer responded spontaneously to the topic proposed or has he/she supplied a "prepared" answer?

Has the writer tried to compose in a dialect or convention of English that he/she speaks with less than facility?

Are his/her errors the result of nervousness, carelessness in composing, carelessness in proofreading, ignorance, or indifference?

Is it legitimate to draw any inference about an author or his/her writing ability without definitive answers to the preceding questions?

* * *

Can you invent a "testing" procedure that could provide a teacher with definitive answers to all of the questions on this page?

Section IV: For Teachers of Writing

The decision to write about the person I know named Tex was not an easy one, except that to me Tex will always be an interesting person. I first met Tex in 1963, in that year he was a Jehovahs' Witness convert and trying to encourage others to be the same. Tex and I were always in some kind of religious argument and debate through the years of 1963 and 1964, and if I had known anything about him them, I would have avoided his company…	The decision to write about a person that I call tex was not an easy choice accept that to me tex will always be an interesting person. I first met Tex in 1963, in that year he was a Jehovah's Witness convert and trying to encourage others to be the same. When ever anyone saw Tex and me we were always in some kind of religious debate, especially through the year 1963 and 1964. If I'd known anything about him then I would have avoided his company…

The passage on the left is a first draft, the one of the right is from the paper actually turned in to the teacher. The teacher marked eight mistakes. He did not, of course, ask the student whether what he had turned in was a first draft or a "corrected" version. Nor did he ask the student for his response to the corrections.

It was the day of June 7, 1974. My team and I had a big game that day. The team we were to play against was consisters to be a better team than we. First we started out with the regular warm up before the game. There was a big crowd on hand ….	These entrepid crimals on the street are getting bolder and bolder everyday. They just won't show no respect for a police officer. The other day when on my regular five hour bet I encountered a crime in the making…

The passage on the left represents a writer's attempt to compose, edit, and proofread at the same time. The one on the right, by the same author and written on the same day, shows him composing and leaving until later questions of spelling, punctuation, and proofreading.

Studying Writers 2

Observing students actively engaged in writing, can you detect the presence of any of the following behaviors:

Laborious composing so that a single sentence may not be completed for several minutes

Starting over each time a mistake is detected

Brief periods of composing followed by more extensive bouts of recopying

The writer's lips move but the pencil does not

The entire paper is reread prior to each new sentence

Furious bouts of writing followed by destruction of what was composed

Constant erasing and self-correction

Extensive pauses between each word and/or phrase

Extensive writing of notes and outlines prior to producing a very brief manuscript

Watching the teacher rather than composing

* * *

Can any of the behaviors listed above be related to any of the following linguistic features in *particular instances*? Can several different behaviors produce the same feature? Can the same behavior produce several different features?

Inconsistency in tense/subject-verb agreement, etc.

Omission of words, particularly prepositions

Repetitiousness

Absence of polysyllabic words

Absence of compound and complex sentence patterns

Run-on sentences

Sentence fragments

Incoherence

Extreme brevity

"Corrections" that impoverish the text

* * *

Observing the same students' oral speech, are any of these behaviors or linguistic features shared by *both* writing and talking?

Studying Writers 3

Determine, on the basis of direct observation, whether any of these phenomena ever occur in your classes:

Writing that represents an impoverishment of the author's spoken speech in terms of vocabulary, sentence length and complexity, content, etc.

Errors in writing that *never* occur in the same person's oral speech

Errors that, if pointed to silently, are spontaneously corrected by the author

Errors that the author spontaneously corrects when the text is read aloud—exactly as it is written—by someone else

Errors that the author can only locate and correct if they are identified by name (e.g., "run-on sentence," "comma splice," etc.)

Errors that continue to appear with the same frequency *after* they have been identified and explained to the author by the teacher.

Can any of the phenomena listed above be related to any of the following in *particular instances*? (You may need to interview the authors in order to find out.)

Carelessness, indifference

Carelessness that occur without the person even knowing that he/she is careless

Functioning in English as a native speaker without ever listening to oneself or noticing the extent of one's vocabulary, length of sentences, etc.

Functioning in English as a native speaker yet approaching writing as if it required knowledge of another language

Attempting to understand written English through an intellectual grasp of grammatical principles rather than a functioning proficiency in the spoken language.

* * *

Studying Writers 4

Ask your students to comment on the following questions in the light of their experience as writers.

> Is it generally possible to write with facility in a mode of English you do not normally speak?
>
> Is it ever the case that "school writing" asks you to express yourself in modes of English you do not normally speak?
>
> Are there any modes of English you do not normally speak in which you *can* compose (orally or in writing) with facility if you wish? Can you, for example, spontaneously express yourself in the style of a television commentator, sportscaster, situation comedy character, or preacher?
>
> To the extent that you *are* able to express yourself in modes of English that are not the same as your normal speech, how have you educated yourself to do this? Through reading? Listening?

* * *

Ask your students to talk to you aloud, on an assigned topic, in the mode or convention of English you wish them to adopt in their formal written work.

> Are they able to "talk like an essay" spontaneously?
>
> Do you find any correlation, in individual cases, between their oral performance in this exercise and their performance in writing in a similar mode?

* * *

Ask your students to listen to recorded or broadcast examples of the kind of English they wish to emulate in their writing. Then invite them to practice spontaneous improvisation in the same mode.

> Are they able to progress as speakers through this exercise?
>
> Do they find that they are able to improvise in modes of English they cannot analyze or describe with precision?
>
> Do they find that they are able to write down what they say in their improvisations?
>
> Do they find that they are able to progress in writing in new modes of English through this procedure, even though their facility may outstrip spelling and punctuation?

Studying Writers 5

Ask your students about their experience as writers in the light of the following questions:

Have you proceeded on the assumption that what teachers care most about are spelling and punctuation? If so, has this influenced your process of writing?

Have you assumed that "correctness" is the first requirement for any writer under any circumstances? If so, how has this influenced your ways of working? Have you ever tested this assumption by handing in a thoughtful paper that contained many mistakes?

Have you assumed that the "best" papers are those that have been most extensively rewritten? If so, have you tested this assumption by asking your teacher to read and compare your successive drafts?

Have you assumed that it is illegitimate to use "I" or to state your own opinions in formal writing? If so, have you questioned your instructors to make sure that they *all* share this view?

Have you assumed that "creative writing" is less acceptable and less demanding than other kinds? If so, have you any experience to support this belief?

Have you assumed that essays are the only kind of writing that can help you build and improve your skills as a writer? Is so, have you any experience to support this belief?

Have you assumed that teachers and professional writers find the practice of writing pleasurable and easy? If so, have you ever conducted any inquiries to find out if this is true?

Have you assumed that the writing of teachers and professional writers is free from errors and need not be revised much in order to serve the purposes to which it is put? Have you ever conducted any inquiries to find out if this is true?

Have you assumed that a writer always composes with other people in mind, never merely to express himself or herself? If so, have you ever conducted any inquiries to find out if this is true?

Do you think that your future progress as a writer could be enhanced by freeing yourself from your preconceptions about authorship and literary expression?

Studying Writers 6

Collect information from your students that bears on the following questions:

Have you every experienced change or improvement in your own writing?

If changes/improvements did occur, were they temporary or permanent?

How did the change/improvement come to your attention? Was it pointed out to you by someone else? Did you notice it *while* you were writing? After examining your own work?

Could you say that there is any correlation between the way in which you became aware of a change and its permanency? Are the changes that are brought to your attention by others more or less permanent than those you detect yourself?

Have you ever felt, as you were working, that your ability as a writer had improved even though you couldn't detect any difference in the product and your teachers continue to award the same grades? If so, was this because you were mistaken? Is it conceivable that changes may be "felt" by the writer long before they become visible in his or her work?

Have you ever experienced a continuing sense of inner change, without visible effect, that was followed at some later point by a sudden and mysterious improvement, visible both to you and your teachers? If so, do you have any explanation for this phenomenon?

Have you ever found changes in your writing taking place literally "overnight," after you have slept between one day's writing activity and the next? If so, have you any explanation for this phenomenon?

Studying Writers 7

Collect information from your students that bears on the following questions:

What are the kinds of assignments and topics that arouse inhibitions?

Which are the topics that appear to be "inhibition-free"?

Which are the kinds of writing (e.g., narrative, dialogue, description, etc.) that are the easiest to start, continue, and bring to a conclusion?

Which are the kinds of writing that one can most easily extend and expand?

Are there areas of your own experience that are so rich they are difficult to write about?

Are there areas of your own experience you can only write about at length if no one else is allowed to read what you say?

Do you ever find you can write more on a highly restricted topic than when you are allowed complete freedom in choosing what you want to say?

Are you more easily mobilized by a picture, a film, or a story written by someone else? Which of these seems to provide you with the most material for your own writing?

Do you find that you have more to say when you write about your opinions or your perceptions?

Do you know, on the basis of experience, whether you perform best as a poet, novelist, essayist, letter writer, etc.? Have you explored enough different kinds of writing to know where your "natural inclinations" are?

Do you pay any attention to the comments written on your papers other than to find out whether the teacher's judgement is favorable or unfavorable?

Do marks on your papers help you to improve? If so, what evidence can you give to show that this is true?

Do you gain more from rewriting to correct your mistakes or starting something new?

Which is more valuable, feedback from the teacher or the responses of other students in the class? Explain your answer.

Studying Writers 8

Ask your students how they would wish you to respond to each of the following sets of alternatives:

To notice what they do or what they don't do

To judge improvement in relation to past performance or perfection

To view mistakes and errors as indications of where work needs to be done or as a means for discriminating between "good" and "bad" students

To care about them or the papers they write